Dear Reader:

The book you a̶̶̶̶̶̶̶̶̶̶̶̶̶̶̶̶̶̶̶ from the St. Martin's True Crime Library, the imprint the *New York Times* calls "the leader in true crime!" Each month, we offer you a fascinating account of the latest, most sensational crime that has captured the national attention. St. Martin's is the publisher of bestselling true crime author and crime journalist Kieran Crowley, who explores the dark, deadly links between a prominent Manhattan surgeon and the disappearance of his wife fifteen years earlier in THE SURGEON'S WIFE. Suzy Spencer's BREAKING POINT guides readers through the tortuous twists and turns in the case of Andrea Yates, the Houston mother who drowned her five young children in the family's bathtub. In Edgar Award-nominated DARK DREAMS, legendary FBI profiler Roy Hazelwood and bestselling crime author Stephen G. Michaud shine light on the inner workings of America's most violent and depraved murderers. In the book you now hold, TWISTED, veteran true crime investigator John Glatt looks at the highly unusual double life of a trusted doctor who murdered his wife.

St. Martin's True Crime Library gives you the stories behind the headlines. Our authors take you right to the scene of the crime and into the minds of the most notorious murderers to show you what really makes them tick. St. Martin's True Crime Library paperbacks are better than the most terrifying thriller, because it's all true! The next time you want a crackling good read, make sure it's got the St. Martin's True Crime Library logo on the spine—you'll be up all night!

Charles E. Spicer

Charles E. Spicer, Jr.
Executive Editor, St. Martin's True Crime Library

A TWISTED LOVE

Richard slowed down, turning left onto Hull Street and parking at the end of the long driveway to Karen's house.

Turning off his headlights, he got out of the car, reaching into the back seat for the heavy loaded rifle, and closing the door as softly as possible. Then he walked up the football field-length driveway toward the house. He could see lights in the windows of the lavish two-story colonial, and hear voices.

All the anger and resentment over what Karen had done to him welled up inside his stomach with each step towards the house. She had to die for the crimes of taking his money and his children, and daring to leave him. Even now, as he approached her house gripping a loaded rifle, he loved her more than anything in his miserable world. But it was a twisted love. Not love in the normal sense of the word. He knew he had to destroy both of their lives, as it was far better for her to be dead than to live a life apart from him . . .

TWISTED

The Secret Desires and Bizarre Double Life of Dr. Richard Sharpe

John Glatt

St. Martin's Paperbacks

FOR ANNETTE WITHERIDGE

TWISTED

Copyright © 2003 by John Glatt.

Cover photograph courtesy AP/Wide World.

ISBN: 0-312-97928-2

Printed in the United States of America

St. Martin's Paperbacks edition / January 2003

10 9 8 7 6 5 4 3 2 1

CONTENTS

ACKNOWLEDGMENTS

This book is the result of more than a year's work and intensive interviews with many of the key people involved in the case. I owe a great debt of gratitude to the Hatfield family, who cooperated with me fully with my research. Especially helpful was Karen's sister Kathleen Lembo and brother Jamie, who painfully relived their memories of Karen's childhood and her courtship by Richard Sharpe. I was also helped by Karen's father, John Hatfield Sr., and elder brother, John Jr. Unfortunately after several telephone calls the Sharpes' daughter Shannon declined to be interviewed for this book.

I would also like to thank Jacob Atwood and his staff of Mark Smith and Erin Shapiro for their continuing patience and help through the project and arranging my initial introduction to the family. I am also grateful to Assistant D.A. Bob Weiner for all his help.

Much gratitude is also owed to: Dr. Keith Ablow, Connie Behnke, Karen Beswick, Chuck DeLorio, Jacqueline Feeney, Theodore Johnson, Scott Kilman, Denise LeClair, Henry Nash, Chief Andy Shagouri, Desi Smith, Tony Surina, Michelle Trioli and Eugene Woolfe.

As always I would like to thank my editor at St. Martin's Press, Charles Spicer, and his team, Joseph Cleemann, Joshua Rivkin and Anderson Bailey, and my agent, Peter Miller and Nathan Rice.

Thanks also to: Susan Chenery, Roger Hitts, Daphna Inbar, Danny and Allie Trachtenberg, Cari Pokrassa, Benny Sporano, Virginia Randall and Wensley Clarkson.

In addition to my own interviews, I was able to draw on helpful and informative broadcast source material from "Dateline NBC" on May 14, 2002 and Court TV's gavel-to-gavel coverage of the trial of Dr. Richard Sharpe in November 2001.

PROLOGUE

Karen Sharpe gazed at her reflection in the full-length mirror. Tonight she was finally free. In a brand-new outfit and carefully applied make-up, she was beautiful. Her radiance erased the worry lines from her face and the mental scars of her violent and deeply troubled marriage.

The vivacious 44-year-old mother of three walked across the expensive rugs in the lobby of her new $650,000 colonial house, lovingly decorated with such hope for the future. Then she walked out the double doors into the warm summer evening, anticipating her new life and the happiness so long denied her.

As usual Karen had planned the evening of July 14, 2000, which would consist of a dinner and cruise, right down to the last detail. And for once her estranged husband Dr. Richard Sharpe—with whom she was presently embroiled in an ugly divorce proceeding—would not be there to spoil it for her, as was his habit.

She had even hired a babysitter named Kristen Dormitzer, to look after her two younger children, Michael, 7, and Alexandra, 4, which was unprecedented, as she rarely went out socially. Tonight, she had told friends, she was determined to sparkle.

After being trapped in twenty-seven years of marital hell—in which she'd suffered broken bones and untold humiliations—she had finally escaped her husband's brutal yoke. And like a prisoner walking free from a life sentence, she was determined to savor her first night of freedom. To help her celebrate what she was calling her "coming-out party," she had invited her younger brother Jamie, who had driven down from Rhode Island with his girlfriend Christine Reagan and her little daughter Aurora, and some of her closest friends to join her.

Since moving to the swanky Massachusetts town of Wenham a few months earlier, her irrepressible good humor and bubbly personality had won her many new friends. But her optimistic, upbeat attitude belied the horrendous secret of a torturous marriage to one of the area's most respected doctors, an unstable, volatile man who was her complete opposite.

Dark and brooding and given to uncontrolled fits of violence, Dr. Richard Sharpe was a self-made millionaire who had earned 5 million dollars from his various dermatology businesses. As far back as 1973, during the first week of their marriage, he had hurled an alarm clock at her face after he had overslept. And things had only gone downhill from there.

Over the years he had beaten her body black-and-blue, and his constant mental cruelty and verbal abuse had robbed her of any self-esteem. He had also abused their daughter Shannon, now 27 years old, when she was growing up.

A heavy drinker who self-medicated with a cocktail of prescription medicines, the 45-year-old doctor was also a transvestite, who got turned on by dressing in his daughter's underwear, even swallowing Karen's birth control pills to sprout womanly breasts on his slender body. This bizarre behavior had left Karen scratching her head, wondering if her husband contemplated a sex change operation to become a woman.

The final straw came after he began staying out all night in drag, refusing to say where he'd been. One morning he had arrived home in full make-up, flaunting himself in front of their young son Michael. Karen was so shocked she had taken her two young children and walked out of the marriage. A furious Dr. Sharpe had reacted by threatening to kill her and her family, so she had gone to court to obtain a restraining order against him.

But on this beautiful mid-summer evening, as she drove Jamie and Christine to the Gull Seafood Restaurant in West Gloucester, she was determined to put all thoughts of the divorce out of her mind.

All through dinner, with her friends Steve and Carol Figurido and Mike and Cynthia Goodhew, Karen's cell phone had rung. It sent a black cloud over the proceedings, as Karen looked at the all-too-familiar digits of her estranged husband's number. Laughing it off, Karen let it ring, explaining that he now called so often, she had started taking her phone off the hook.

After dinner, the party proceeded to the harbor where the brand new, state-of-the-art Hurricane whale cruiser, which Karen's friend Ronnie Goulat had charted for his annual employee party, gently swayed in the calm waters. Each year he invited Karen, but this was the first time she had ever accepted and he was delighted for her.

It was a picture-perfect evening as the Hurricane slipped anchor, gently sailing out of Gloucester Harbor. A full moon smiled down through a light haze, caressing the shimmering waters, as the large whale-watcher embarked on the night cruise.

On deck Karen stared blissfully at the receding historic harbor, a radiant smile lighting up her face. Below deck a seventies cover-band played old favorites, as Karen danced the night away, as if she didn't have a care in the world.

"For the first time I saw her let her guard down and enjoy herself," said long-time friend Sonia Frontiero, who was also on the cruise. "She left Richard and was just finally trying to get on with her life."

The open bar was doing brisk business, but Karen, who never touched alcohol, stuck to soda. And towards the end of the cruise, she slipped a white sweater over her navy paisley blouse, and went out on deck to chat with Jamie.

The brother and sister had an exceptionally close relationship, and Jamie knew how difficult the divorce had been for her. But in the last conversation they would ever have, Karen seemed more optimistic than he had ever seen her, as she spoke about her future, well away from the clutches of Dr. Richard Sharpe.

The Hurricane docked at 11:00 p.m. and after saying goodbye to the Figuridos and the Goodhews, Karen drove Jamie and Christine two exits east on Route 128 to Wenham. Then, as they were pulling into the driveway of 19 Hull Street, Karen's cell phone rang, sending a shiver down her spine. She looked down at the number, breathing a sigh of relief on seeing her own home number.

It was the babysitter, Kristen, who had been accidentally scratched on her cornea by little Aurora. The young student had applied ice-packs to her swelling eye, but was still in great pain. Karen, a trained nurse, assured her she'd take care of her as soon as she got back.

A couple of minutes later, Karen rushed through the front doors, immediately taking control of the situation.

As Jamie and Christine went into the TV room to see the children, Karen examined Kristen's eye, applying a saline solution to ease the pain, and made another ice-pack. Then she decided that Kristen needed to go to the emergency room, and prepared to drive her there.

At 11:40 p.m. Kristen was standing a few feet away from the front double doors waiting for Karen, when one of them opened a fraction, revealing the white, ghostly face of Dr. Richard Sharpe.

"Is Karen here?" he asked calmly.

Although she had never met the doctor, Kristen instantly realized who the pasty-faced individual was. Then she saw Karen come out of the kitchen and walk towards her husband, as Jamie and Christine looked up from the other side of the foyer.

"Richard, you shouldn't be here," admonished Karen, shooing him away with her hand.

"Oh my God," she screamed a few seconds later, as he kicked the door fully open, revealing a rifle aimed straight at her chest.

She tried to run away . . .

Chapter One

RAGE OF THE FATHER

Richard John Sharpe was born on August 23, 1954, in Derby, Connecticut, the third son of toolmaker Benjamin Sharpe and his homemaker wife, Laura. Their first son Robert had been born fourteen years earlier, and their second son Ben followed in 1945. Fifteen months after Richard was born, his mother gave birth to a girl they christened Laurie, to complete the family. A hard worker, Benjamin seldom came home until late at night, and worked weekends, never turning down overtime— he needed the extra income to pay off his gambling debts.

The smallest city in Connecticut, Derby was established as a trading post in 1642 and rests at the intersection of the Naugatuck and Housatonic Rivers, in the southwest corner of the state. The city's early prosperity came from manufacturing industries, and the opening of the Housatonic Dam in 1870 attracted a wealth of new industry.

After the Second World War the factories moved south, attracted by cheaper labor, and thousands of jobs disappeared. By the 1950s the city was fighting to survive, but Benjamin Sharpe's skills as a toolmaker/electrician always put food on the table for his family.

When Richard was a young boy, his father moved the family across the Housatonic River to nearby Shelton. He bought a house at 36 Soundview Avenue, across the road from the Harry B. Brownson Country Club, with its immaculate golf course. The Sharpes lived in the comparatively ritzy Huntington section, but by the time they arrived, the town was well past its prime, a fading shadow of the industrial powerhouse it had been at the turn of the century, with asphalt now the major industry.

Derby's natural twin, Shelton was named after Edward Shelton, founder of America's first tack factory in 1836. But after industry moved out during the Depression, the town never recovered. When Richard Sharpe was growing up in the 1950s, run-down factories littered the predominantly blue-collar farming community. It had a claustrophobic small-town atmosphere, where everyone knew everyone, and there were few prospects for advancement for ambitious young people, who seldom stayed long after leaving school.

Benjamin Sharpe personified the frustrations of Shelton. He was a compulsive gambler who dreamed of winning a ticket out of town. He often drank to excess and on the rare occasions he came home, usually drunk and in a bad mood, he'd terrorize his family both physically and mentally, calling his sons "stupid," "dumb fucks" and "worthless bastards," mainly venting his anger on his eldest son Robert.

"My father was unique," Robert would later explain. "[He] harassed my mother and he beat me up."

When Richard was four years old his brother Bob couldn't take it anymore and left home at the age of eighteen and got married. Six years later he divorced, moving next door to his grandfather Michael Sharpe's house. He started a small business repairing televisions and radios. As a young child, Richard would often go over there to learn electronics.

"He was actually more of a father than my father was," said Richard. "Once he helped me build a science project."

When Richard was ten years old he was traumatized after witnessing his father repeatedly smashing a heavy metal poker across Robert's head during a violent outburst at their grandfather's house.

"He almost killed me," said Robert, who remembered being covered in blood from the resulting deep head wound, "for no reason at all."

Benjamin beat Richard with a baseball bat, and reportedly chased him around the house with a gun.

Benjamin Sharpe also verbally abused their mother, who had a seizure disorder. She always tried to keep the peace in the household, and protect the children against their father's anger, by jumping in between them during physical fights. But Sharpe also employed psychological warfare to wear down his wife and children.

"He would just gnaw," said Robert. "He'd take a subject with my mother and he'd just pick at her, and she'd just take it. I'd be in bed and he'd pick on me. He'd pick on Richie and he'd pick on all of us so he'd be late for work in the morning."

But the whole Sharpe family was traumatized when Richard's grandfather, a deeply religious man with severe psychiatric problems, hanged himself. Later Richard would maintain he also suffered from mental instability, saying it ran in his family.

There was little money in the Sharpe household, due to their father's gambling, and the family never went on vacation, except for an occasional trip to visit relatives in Brooklyn.

Growing up, Richard idolized his brother Ben, who left home at nineteen and married a year later, moving to California. Seven-year-old Richard had dreamed of going to the West Coast with him, and was distraught when their mother refused to let him go.

"I started calling him two, three or four times a day," Richard would remember. "I begged his wife to let me come out."

But when his father got the phone bill he was furious, ordering him to stop making long-distance calls to his brother.

"So I actually took a rare coin collection that my grandfather had given me and went down to the pay phone to make long-distance calls to California," he said.

After his brothers left home, Richard found himself taking the brunt of his father's anger. And although the boy desperately wanted his father to be proud of him, he found himself being continually insulted and mentally abused instead.

The only member of the family to escape Benjamin Sharpe's wrath was his daughter Laurie. Richard became obsessively jealous of her. When he was ten years old he began locking himself in the bathroom to escape his father's "ranting and raving." "He wouldn't break the door down, because then he'd have to fix it," Richard remembered. One day he saw his sister's clothes in the laundry hamper and put them on. He felt so good wearing Laurie's underwear and dresses that he would often dress up and sit in the corner of the bathroom, pretending to be her, every time his father went on a tirade.

"[I] actually felt more relaxed and safer dressed like that," Richard would later say.

Over the next few years his cross-dressing escalated from once a month to almost every day. And when he was twelve he used the money he'd earned from selling golf balls to buy his first complete set of female clothes.

"I remember going to a store and buying an outfit," he said. "I always had long hair when I was a kid, so I combed my hair a little differently. I put the outfit on and I actually went out in public, because I was so convincing. And that was the beginning of that."

Ultimately he was caught in drag by his father, who hit him.

"He didn't say anything about the cross-dressing, but he yelled at me for taking my sister's clothes. [He said] if he caught me with her clothes anymore, I'd be in trouble."

Another means of escape for Richard was sleeping over at friends' houses or staying out until the early hours of the morning. He became wild and unruly, often skipping school and getting poor grades. He would use his spare time working for his brother Robert or doing odd-jobs for his best friend Frank Pelaggi's father.

Frank, who was in Richard's class at Shelton High School, often visited the Sharpe home, where the two boys would build go-carts. He witnessed Benjamin Sharpe's furious temper and verbal abuse on numerous occasions.

"He used to call [Richard] a 'miserable fucking bastard' and [tell him] to get out of the house, as he was no good," said Pelaggi. "He said teenagers should be put in a bottle and shipped off to war. It was intense."

When Richard was twelve, his brother Ben returned from California. Richard moved in with him for six months to escape his troubled home life. Having hardly seen his kid brother during the seven years he'd been away, Ben found him "an aggressive teenager" who was being persecuted by their father.

Ben set up a computer consulting business, offering Richard a part-time job in his office and the opportunity to learn computers. Although his school grades were dismal, as he rarely attended classes, Richard discovered a natural ability for computers and science. Indeed, several years earlier in grade school he had surprised his mother by winning first prize in a science fair organized by a local radio station. Laura Sharpe was so proud she wrote Ben in California, saying how smart Richard was, and that he had a great future.

One day while they were working in the office, Richard would later testify, Ben happened to pick up the phone and overheard his wife arranging a date at a hotel with a contractor friend. Ben was furious, driving Richard with him to borrow a handgun. They then went to the hotel with the gun to confront the lovers, but the contractor managed to talk his way out of the situation. The two brothers left without a shot being fired.

It was the first time Richard had ever seen a gun, but it wouldn't be the last.

In his early teens, Richard began to fight back when his father attacked him. Father and son would wrestle each other to the floor, and soon Benjamin began to back off, realizing that Richard was now big enough to hold his own. At school Richard began getting confrontational, deliberately provoking fights with his schoolmates, and usually coming out on the losing end.

"I was the little shrimp, and the bullies used to pick on me," he said. "The fights would flare and I just wouldn't back down even if they were twice my size. I inevitably got my butt kicked to the point where it was almost a joke."

But Richard didn't confine his fighting to school bullies, and began beating up his little sister Laurie, also a pupil at Shelton High School. Although they were just fifteen months apart, Richard and his sister never played together. Laurie always felt he was jealous of her for being a girl.

"He was very physically and emotionally abusive to me even in grade school," she would later remember. "And he abused our mother, who was pretty much your Kool-Aid mom, and very good to him."

On one occasion, when his mother failed to crease his pants to his satisfaction, Richard lashed out, calling her a "slut, a scumbag and a prostitute." But mild-mannered Laura Sharpe just took the abuse in her stride, never attempting to punish him.

"From elementary on up he seemed to get worse," said Laurie. "He got more aggressive, more bizarre."

Once, as a joke, he urinated in his brother Ben's bottle of wine and then put the cork back in, waiting for him to drink it. Another time at elementary school, after Laurie had been given a note to take home to their mother about Richard's bad behavior, he savagely beat her up inside the principal's office, before snatching the note away.

He was also angry that his sister's bedroom was bigger than his and that she had a stereo system. In revenge he began stealing her stuff and reportedly killing her pets. Laurie was so traumatized by his erratic behavior that she put ten locks on her bedroom door to keep him out. But even then he tried to break it down.

Paradoxically, although his parents attempted to keep him away from the family pets, if any of them took sick he would treat them. Although he had little or no medical knowledge, little Richard would always be able to cure whatever was wrong.

Even Laurie, who always feared her brother as a child, would later credit him for saving her life at the age of ten.

"I was lying on the couch complaining of a sore

throat," she remembered. "My mom didn't deem this condition serious, [but then] Richard walked in the door, looked at me, and ran to get a flashlight and thermometer."

The twelve-year-old took his sister's temperature, looked down her throat and pressed on her neck, declaring, "We need to get Laurie to the emergency room. She has a severe case of strep."

According to Laurie, an ER doctor later told their mother that her brother had probably saved her life, as she could have died if she had not received treatment in time.

All through his schooling, Richard was always in trouble for skipping classes and getting into fights. At the age of fifteen he had his first brush with the law, after getting drunk on beer and going for a joyride in a car his brother Robert had rented. He was picked up by the Shelton police and was given a stern warning.

"I got thrown out of the house by my father," remembered Richard. "My mother wanted me back and there was a lot of friction. I was just a mess during that whole period."

His father finally relented and let him move back into the house, but his behavior went from bad to worse.

During his high school years Richard's temper often veered out of control. He began hanging out with a wild set of friends and drinking alcohol. Frank Pelaggi's father had a full bar stocked with liquor in the basement, and the two boys would often raid it on weekends, sitting around drinking and listening to loud rock music.

Richard had recently saved enough money from his odd-jobs to buy an old 1969 Mustang which he totally rebuilt and souped up, proudly driving it around Shelton. The nerdy-looking teenager grew his hair long, and started hanging around with a clique called the "Gear

Heads," who loved tinkering around with cars.

"Everybody liked [Richard's] car," said Frank Pelaggi. "It was bright red with scoops on the front."

Like many 1970s Shelton teenagers, Richard frequented the Bradley Parking Lot tailgate parties, which usually culminated in everyone jumping into their cars to race to New York City, where the drinking age was eighteen.

Richard was now getting more popular and his mother encouraged him to bring new friends back to the house, where she would bake them cookies and brownies.

"The town was like *Happy Days*," said Tony Surina, who was a year ahead of Sharpe at school and is now a Shelton policeman. "Everybody knew everybody here and Rich didn't particularly stand out."

Richard also befriended a long-haired boy who went by the name "Hippie," and turned him on to marijuana.

"We'd sit around in his attic, which was complete with a black lamp, beads and lava lamps," Richard remembered. "We smoked pot and occasionally hash."

Sharpe now became interested in girls, discovering that many were attracted to his feminine features. Years later he would boast of once having three girls in Shelton High School fighting over him. Although he loved the thrill of wearing women's clothes, he was attracted to women and otherwise heterosexual.

In the spring of 1972 Richard and two friends, Tommy Mulready and Tommy Rivas, were on their way to an English class when they spotted a hot new sixteen-year-old student named Karen Hatfield, who was in her very first week at Shelton High. They followed her up the stairs, crudely remarking about her skin-tight jeans which had a patch on the back pocket saying, "built not stuffed."

Finally, as they were going down the hall, Richard

plucked up the courage to ask if the patch referred to her or the jeans. Karen visibly blushed as the three boys started laughing, but stopped to introduce herself anyway. She explained that she had taken the patch from an old mattress and sewn it on her jeans, thinking it was cool.

Complimenting her on her sense of humor, Richard escorted her to the English class, making a point of sitting next to her. With her big brown eyes, and heart-shaped face framed by long dark hair, Richard considered her to be *the* most beautiful girl at Shelton High. From then on, he would make a point of attending every English class, as he embarked on a mission to make Karen his own.

Chapter Two

KAREN

If Richard Sharpe's upbringing was unstable and volatile, Karen Hatfield's was just the opposite. Her parents, John and Patricia Hatfield, were devoted to their five children, providing a secure grounding that would be the envy of any child.

Karen, who was the oldest, was born on October 3, 1955, in Mount Clemens, Michigan. Dubbed "America's Bath City," the healing mineral springs were discovered in 1862, drawing arthritis sufferers from all over the world to the forty bathhouses that flourished up to the Second World War.

Karen spent the first few years of her life in Mount Clemens, but from then on the family was constantly on the move, because of John's high-powered executive job as CEO of a multi-national electronics manufacturer.

"Karen was a sweet kid," said her father. "Everybody adored her."

Over the next few years John and Patricia had four more children, John Jr., Kathleen, Jeff and James, who was nine years younger than Karen, and the baby of the family. While they were growing up, their father's demanding job took the Hatfields to Ohio, back to Michigan and finally to Shelton, Connecticut, in the early 1970s.

"We had a wonderful family," said Karen's brother John. "Karen was just a typical kid, but although she was a year ahead of me, we spent most of our times in the same schools."

Karen was a caring sister to her siblings and like a second mother to her youngest brother James, known in the family as Jamie. On his fifth birthday, which fell on Easter that year, his big sister cooked him a special cake with marshmallow bunnies and jelly beans on it.

"She really did a lot as far as things like that for us," he would remember more than a quarter of a century later. "She'd just go out of her way to please anybody."

When Karen was in elementary school in Ohio, she would help disabled children get on and off the school bus. When she left the school, it would give her a special award for her thoughtfulness.

A good student and always near the top of her class with A's and B's, Karen had an ability to make friends and endear herself to people.

"She was able to move into a new school and just make friends off the bat," said her younger sister Kathleen.

But the pressure of having to move around so much as a child, never staying in one town long enough to lay down roots, made her insecure and unsure of herself.

John Hatfield was often away on business, traveling to Europe and Asia, leaving Karen and his wife Patricia to look after the children.

"Karen always took care of everyone," said sister Kathleen. "We moved around a lot as kids, and she always made sure she was looking after everybody at any given time."

The role of big sister to her four younger siblings was something Karen took very seriously. If they were ever bullied at school, she would bake a cake or buy chocolates to cheer them up. She had a natural maternal instinct and her family adored her.

In 1972, at the age of sixteen, Karen moved with her family to Shelton, Connecticut, settling down on Longview Road in the bucolic White Hills area, where the Pootatuck Indians had hunted four centuries earlier.

All the children enrolled in the Shelton schools and Karen, feeling insecure about starting again in a new town, was flattered by the attention Richard Sharpe paid to her. Before long he had provided her an entrée into his social set.

"I met her when she first moved here and came to our school," said Frank Pelaggi. "Karen was a friend of mine too."

Straight after their first meeting, Richard ditched two girls he had been seeing and began courting Karen. Shy and unsure of himself, the gangly seventeen-year-old high school senior plucked up the courage to invite her to an upcoming high school dance. She accepted, but said she had already promised to go with a boy named Joey Aldo. Richard immediately offered to drive her there in his cool red Mustang and Karen accepted his offer.

At the appointed time he arrived at Longview Road decked out in his best clothes. They spent most of the night driving around Shelton in the Mustang, as he told her of his dreams and ambitions for the future. They almost missed the dance, finally arriving fifteen minutes before the end.

"And from that point we were going steady," Sharpe would later explain. "Karen and I were dating."

Over the next few weeks Richard became a familiar

sight at the Hatfield house, picking Karen up for school and then dropping her off late at night. But John Hatfield did not approve of his daughter's scruffy, long-haired new boyfriend. "He looked like a slob at that time," said Hatfield. "Long hair and raggedy-looking." He especially objected to Richard's insistence that the couple drive to and from school together.

The first time John Hatfield set eyes on Richard was when he arrived unannounced at their front door at 9:00 p.m. with two friends in tow looking for Karen. Her father told him she was out on a date. Richard slunk off, looking dejected and John Hatfield forgot about it. But within days his daughter and Richard became inseparable and Hatfield became extremely concerned about their relationship, after hearing that Richard seldom attended school and was a troublemaker.

"He wanted Karen to do things that were against our basic beliefs," he said. "We wanted her to take the bus because he had a bad reputation."

But when Hatfield put his foot down, forbidding Karen from riding to school in his Mustang, Richard challenged him, arguing that Karen was sixteen and could do whatever she wanted.

"Although we were against it, we didn't make an issue out of it," said Hatfield. "We didn't put him down."

Richard Sharpe soon became a regular fixture at the Hatfield residence, where he met Karen's three brothers and sister Kathleen, trying to work himself into the family.

"As her only sister I would ask her about Richard," said Kathleen. "I would get a little bit of information about stuff going on in their relationship, but I was only fourteen, so it didn't make a lot of sense."

Initially, Richard engaged Kathleen as an ally, assisting her with her trigonometry homework and generally trying to be helpful around the house.

"I remember him offering to do this and that," said Kathleen. "He was able to do some electrical work."

But Kathleen thought him arrogant and self-obsessed, always trying to outdo everyone. "He didn't like rules," she remembered. "He was always trying to do something that would put him on the map. Something that was going to say, 'Richard Sharpe—Superstar.' "

John Jr. didn't like Richard either and kept out of his way, and little Jamie, just seven at the time, sensed tension in the air whenever Karen's new boyfriend visited.

"I know my parents weren't happy with the situation," remembered Jamie. "There was turmoil between him and my parents, which made me not care for him right off the bat."

But Karen was smitten with him and refused to end the relationship, and even began uncharacteristically skipping classes to be with him. Whenever she babysat for neighbors to make extra money, Richard would come around, so they could spend the evening together. On weekends they went out on romantic dates. On the rare nights they couldn't meet he would telephone her at home and they would talk late into the night. When they fell asleep they'd leave the line open and carry on talking when they woke up.

Initially, Richard was on his best behavior with Karen and careful to control his violent temper. But once when his sister Laurie was using the phone when he wanted to call his girlfriend, he flew into an uncontrollable rage and hit her, before ripping the phone out of the wall and taking it into his room to make the call.

From the very beginning of their relationship Richard knew how to manipulate Karen and get his way, providing the attention and flattery she needed. Later, she would admit to having little self-confidence as a teenager and Richard cunningly knew how to exploit her weakness.

"He was somebody who was interested in her," said Karen Beswick, who years later became Karen's confidante. "And in those teenage years you are very vulnerable to a lot of things."

In December 1972, during her senior year of high school, Karen told Richard she had missed a period. He immediately took charge, taking her down to a Planned Parenthood clinic for a pregnancy test, which proved positive. For the first few months Karen hid her pregnancy from her parents, knowing they would be horrified. She went to a doctor who gave her some vitamins and tried to prepare her for pregnancy.

Although Karen started wearing loose clothes to hide her expanding belly, she eventually had no alternative but to 'fess up, after her mother began asking why she was gaining so much weight.

"We weren't thrilled at the time," said her father. "But we left it up to Karen to decide what to do, and she made her decision."

Ultimately her father removed Karen from Shelton High School to save further embarrassment, hiring a home tutor to help her graduate in her final semester.

Sharpe would later claim that Karen's parents gave them little support, urging Karen to give up the baby for adoption and even arranging a meeting at Catholic Family Planning.

"I think Karen planned to put the baby up for adoption," claimed Richard years later. "We were talking about how they had these great homes. But as the pregnancy progressed we were talking more and more about getting married, but we didn't know how we were going to do it. Then I started taking care of it and actually started getting serious."

But his imminent fatherhood did not stop Richard Sharpe from celebrating a so-far lackluster academic career by being crowned Shelton High School's 1973 Prom King. Unfortunately Karen, heavily pregnant at the time, was not there to share in his glory. His official prom queen was a far plainer, bespectacled fellow student.

In the official school prom photograph in the 1973 *Argus* yearbook, Richard is pictured with a large crown, wearing a tuxedo, a bow tie and a large carnation in his lapel. His long, dark bushy hair obscures his left eye, and he has the beginnings of a thin mustache. There is a wry smile on his face, as though he has at last taken his rightful place in the public eye.

Shannon Sharpe was born two months prematurely on May 31, 1973, three weeks before her parents graduated. It was a difficult birth and Karen spent a week in the hospital before the delivery. Still uncertain what to do with their beautiful new baby girl, the new parents decided to call her Shannon, figuring it was an unusual name they could later track down in the event of adoption.

While Karen was in the hospital, the couple discussed marriage, deciding that they both wanted to go to college and continue their studies, so they could get good jobs to support themselves and their daughter. Richard suggested to Karen's father that he fix up their basement and move in with Karen and Shannon. At this point John Hatfield put his foot down and said no.

"He was not thrilled with us because we wouldn't let him move into our house," said Hatfield. "We had four other children at the time and we said, 'No, that won't work.' "

Although Hatfield offered to pay their rent if they found a place, the young parents never took him up on the idea. Hatfield thought Richard irresponsible and told Karen that she was welcome to stay with Shannon, but he would not allow two unmarried teenagers living under his roof, setting a bad example for the younger children.

Baby Shannon spent several weeks in the hospital, too frail to go home. Her parents would visit her there several times a week. They also decided that Karen would keep the baby and they would both continue living with their respective parents.

When Shannon was finally discharged, she and her mother moved into the bedroom Karen had previously shared with her sister Kathleen, who now slept on an old couch in the living room. When Shannon woke up every morning for her 3:00 a.m. feeding, Karen would bring her downstairs to play with Kathleen, until her bottle was ready.

That summer, Richard Sharpe had half-heartedly applied for several colleges, and while he was waiting to hear the outcome, he started a landscaping business, as well as working as an electrician's helper for Frank Pelaggi's father.

"All I did was to try and save money," he would later explain. "And I sold my car."

John Hatfield did not like Richard coming around to see his daughter and new granddaughter and tried to stop all contact between them. Karen too was becoming increasingly concerned about his possessiveness, feeling that he was trying to control her. Every time she went out for a walk with Shannon on Longview Road, Richard was there to meet her. And she told her family that she thought he was spying on the house.

But in late summer, when Richard announced they should get married and be together forever, Karen became frightened, leaving town without telling Richard. Her father said he got a call from Karen one morning, saying she wanted to take Shannon to her Aunt Helen in Waynesburg, just south of Pittsburgh. Hatfield then called his travel agent and made all the arrangements for flights. He drove them to the airport, promising to drive up to Pennsylvania the following week to see them.

But on his return to Shelton, he found Sharpe and a couple of his cronies sitting on a lawn by his house, demanding to know where Karen and Shannon had gone. When he refused to tell him, Richard stormed off.

"I freaked out," Richard said. "I didn't know if I'd ever see her or Shannon again. I couldn't go to work and I was begging her parents to tell me where she was."

Over the next week Richard returned to Longview Road again and again, pleading for information on Karen and Shannon's whereabouts. On one occasion, he and two friends sneaked into the kitchen and stole a day timer. Ironically, when he got home, Richard discovered that Karen had just telephoned his mother, leaving her Pennsylvania phone number.

"I called her back and we talked," said Sharpe. "Then my friends jumped in [a] car and went to Pennsylvania."

They drove 465 miles through the night, arriving at Karen's Aunt Helen's house early the following morning. Then they immediately turned around and drove back to Shelton with Karen and her baby.

On her return, Richard Sharpe would later testify, Karen moved in with the family of a high school friend, to avoid any further friction with her parents over Sharpe. Over the next few weeks Richard worked hard at his landscaping business, managing to save a couple of thousand dollars to put himself through school. He was still living with his parents, so his expenses were minimal, and he began trying to pressure Karen into marriage, saying that they could now afford an apartment and both start school.

Once again Karen attempted to break away from him, starting an affair with the friend. But when Richard found out, he flew into a rage, immediately confronting his rival. Although his rival was far bigger than he was, the weedy Sharpe threatened to beat him up, and punches were exchanged.

"I ended up slapping [Karen] during the argument," he would later testify. "And then we kissed and made up and had a passionate reunion, as we always did."

Taking advantage of the situation, Sharpe once again proposed marriage and this time Karen accepted. On August 20, 1973, they got a marriage license without telling their parents.

Twelve days later on September 1, they were secretly married by a justice of the peace, with three friends and baby Shannon in attendance.

When Karen's family found out, they were livid, fearing that Richard had finally won, craftily manipulating her into marriage, and that they had lost her forever.

"That was tough," remembered Kathleen. "We really felt that she was gone and he'd got her. And although we hoped she was going to be happy, you know that [these things] usually don't turn out very well."

Chapter Three

THE HONEYMOON FROM HELL

Straight after the civil ceremony, Karen and Richard moved into a cheap two-bedroom apartment in Shelton. John Hatfield grudgingly resigned himself to the situation, generously furnishing the newlyweds' apartment with a television, a refrigerator and a playpen for Shannon.

But in the very first week of their marriage Richard showed his true colors, after Karen failed to set the alarm clock and he overslept.

"My husband smashed an alarm clock against the wall due to my failure to wake him up early," Karen would later testify in an affidavit. "Throughout the first few years of our marriage our household was riddled with tension."

Over the next few months Richard's increasingly erratic behavior and fits of anger would often wake up baby Shannon in the middle of the night. Determined to make her marriage work, not wanting to admit defeat to her parents, Karen never complained about the abuse she suffered. She remained with her new husband, however extreme his behavior.

In late 1973, Richard started working full-time for a bachelor's degree in engineering at the University of Bridgeport, while Karen enrolled for several nursing courses at Norwalk Community College. She also found a job in day care to earn some extra money, often taking Shannon along with her.

John Hatfield tried to make the best out of what he considered a bad situation, by helping them out with a little money. But when Sharpe demanded a far larger sum to finance his schooling, and Hatfield refused, he lashed out by refusing to allow Karen and Shannon to see their family.

"That was his method for getting even with us," said Hatfield. "He did the same thing to his mother for a while."

During the first years of their marriage, in a twisted form of blackmail, if he didn't get his own way, Sharpe would often forbid Karen to let her family see their beloved granddaughter.

"It happened a lot at the beginning and was very hurtful," said Kathleen. "We'd call Karen and she'd say, 'I can't come around. You can't see Shannon.' That was his way of manipulating my parents, Karen and the rest of us."

Relations between Sharpe and the Hatfield family had always been cool, but now they turned downright frosty on the rare occasions Sharpe attended family gatherings.

"He didn't talk to us," said Hatfield, "and we couldn't get him into a conversation. So that was that."

At Christmas 1973, John Hatfield extended an olive branch to his new son-in-law, inviting him, along with Karen and Shannon, to a family get-together. While the family exchanged presents under the Christmas tree, he handed Sharpe his gift-wrapped Christmas present.

"We had bought him a couple of shirts," remembered

Hatfield. "He opened them up, looked at them and sneered. Then he threw them aside. That was his method of behaving."

Karen sat in embarrassed silence watching the spectacle, as she would do on so many future family occasions over the years. Later she would discover that her new husband had an almost pathological hatred of Christmas.

She had become immune to his constant taunts, accusing her of being fat and dumb. It was easier for her to sit back and take the abuse, than to risk an argument, and possible violence, if she stood up for herself.

During the early years of their marriage the Sharpes were often broke, existing on student loans and the odd cash he made moonlighting for his brother Bob's computer company. Their main financial support came from Karen, who worked double shifts in day care to put him through school.

Shannon was growing into a delightfully beautiful little girl, with her mother's cherubic face and luscious soft eyes. When he allowed her contact with the Hatfields, her father would have his friends drive her over to their house in the morning and then collect her at night, after they had both finished work.

"Shannon was just adorable," said Kathleen. "We all loved having her around because she was such a great kid."

Almost a year into their marriage, Sharpe viciously hit Karen during an argument and her father found out. John Hatfield was furious and took his son-in-law aside, warning him never to raise a finger against Karen again. For once Sharpe was apologetic, assuring his father-in-law it would never happen again.

But after that incident Karen never let her family

know about the increasing abuse her husband was inflicting on her and Shannon.

"She didn't want to tell us for whatever reason, and I'm sure there were a million of them," said her sister Kathleen. "Was she embarrassed? Was she feeling like she was going to get, 'I told you so'? Possibly. But Karen was always welcome back at any point with open arms and my parents supported her every step of the way. They just wanted her to get rid of him."

In 1976 Sharpe moved his family to another apartment in Ansonia, three miles north of Shelton. By now he was totally out of control, wreaking havoc and misery on his wife and infant daughter, making their lives a nightmare. He was working harder than ever on his degree, and at nights on a computer consulting project for Bob. And the more pressure he put himself under, the worse his temper became.

On one occasion he kept Karen prisoner in their home for more than two days, refusing to let her leave.

"He also began physically abusing me," she would write years later in a sworn affidavit. "On one occasion the abuse was so severe that I pleaded with him to allow me to seek medical care, promising to inform the hospital that I fell down a flight of stairs."

Sharpe finally agreed to take her to the hospital for the injuries he'd caused and while she was being treated, callously whispered in her ear, "I want you to die."

Years later Shannon Sharpe would recall in court papers her earliest memory as seeing her father throw a glass straight into her mother's face, causing a deep cut.

"She immediately ran over to me and carried me into another room," claimed Shannon, "so that I would not continue to witness the abuse."

Richard Sharpe would later recall another argument during this period, while he was working late at his brother's office with a young woman accountant.

". . . about one or two in the morning Karen showed up unexpectedly," he said, "and accused me of having an affair with the [woman]."

A bitter screaming fight ensued and Karen stormed out, saying she was going home to pack her bags and leave with Shannon. Up against a tight deadline, Sharpe carried on working, but could no longer concentrate, worried that she might actually be serious.

After ten minutes he jumped in his car, heading north to Ansonia at breakneck speed, running a stop sign. When a police officer, who witnessed the incident, tried to flag him down, Sharpe refused to stop, accelerating away at high speed.

"I made it back to the apartment," he remembered. "And we were having this big blow-out fight when the police arrived because they had got my license plate."

Sharpe was taken to the Shelton police station and locked up for several hours, eventually charged with several traffic violations and failing to obey a police officer.

"They were trying to figure out whether to [charge me] with something more serious, but they realized it was a heat of passion sort of thing and gave me a break."

Later, Sharpe would play down his violent abuse during the first few years of the marriage, claiming they were mainly "shouting matches," where only rarely things would get thrown.

"On a few occasions it did become physical," he would claim. "And most of the physical stuff was about infidelity on one side or the other, or suggested infidelity."

And although Karen tried to summon up the courage to leave him several times during the first five years of their marriage, she would always return a few hours later, believing Richard's promises to change his behavior.

In the mid-1970s, Sharpe began taking his wife's birth control pills, saying they controlled his vicious temper. A side-effect of the pills was the growth of small, womanly breasts, which didn't seem to bother him. By this time he had told Karen about his long-time fascination with wearing women's clothes. He would later say she indulged him, joining him in sexual games involving cross-dressing. On one occasion, according to him, they even went to a Halloween party dressed as sisters, enjoying a passionate night of lovemaking afterwards.

"One way I relieved severe stress was to cross-dress," he explained. "And I thought that maybe [the estrogen in the pills would also] release stress."

It would be the beginning of an addiction to a cocktail of prescription painkillers and tranquilizers that in time would engulf him.

But however bizarre and erratic his behavior at home, Richard Sharpe managed to impress his professors and fellow students, many of whom considered him a genius. He was a brilliant student, and always at the top of his class.

A young English girl named Dawn Ward, who was in his chemistry class at the University of Bridgeport, became close friends with him during this period.

"I was drawn to him because he was so gifted [and] I can attest to his genius," she said. "One of our professors, who taught full-time at Columbia University in New York, told me that he was the brightest student he had ever taught."

During the two years they studied together in the late 1970s, Ward met Karen, Shannon and Richard's brother Ben Sharpe. Her daughter Sophia would often babysit

Shannon at the Sharpes' Ansonia apartment.

"I got to know Karen, who was a sweet young woman," said Sophia. "I ended up feeling like a family member."

Later, looking back on their friendship, Ward would remember Richard Sharpe as "a loving husband and devoted father," who was never "mean or violent in word or deed."

Sophia also remembers the Sharpe family as "kind and warm," and would later become Richard's staunchest supporter, refusing to believe that he could be capable of any physical abuse.

During his four years at the University of Bridgeport, Sharpe worked around the clock, studying and moonlighting for his brother Bob, rarely having any time for Karen or to be a proper father to Shannon. He seemed unable to relate to his beautiful little daughter and would never play games or read to her. Before long, he began physically abusing Shannon too.

Years later she would compare her miserable childhood to terrorism. And although Sharpe loved to describe himself as a family man, claiming that his children were the most important thing in his life, Shannon believed he only used her to get Karen's attention. She felt they had no natural father–daughter relationship, and he would always insist she call him "Richard."

"My childhood was a state of constant fear in which I could not predict what would cause Richard's temper to escalate," Shannon would later testify. "I cannot recall the first instance in which Richard was physically abusive toward me, because the abuse is longer than my memory."

Chapter Four

MONSTER

In 1978 Richard Sharpe received his bachelor's degree in mechanical engineering, chemistry and physics, immediately enrolling for a two-year master's degree night course at Rensselaer Polytechnic Institute at the Hartford Graduate Center.

Things were finally looking up financially for the Sharpes, with Richard making good money as a mechanical engineer for United Technologies, as well as his part-time computer consulting jobs. They moved to a bigger apartment in Hartford, Connecticut, and Karen also found herself a position as a registered nurse in a local doctor's office. For the first time since their marriage there was money coming into the household.

Fired with enthusiasm after sailing through his bachelor's degree, Sharpe now felt confident enough to try to fulfill his life-long ambition to become a doctor. For the next two years he and Karen would put all their energies into him passing his masters, so he could qualify for medical school.

"We actually got ahead of the curve," he would later remember. "I'd always wanted to be a doctor, but having not done so well at school, I initially thought it was beyond my reach. Now I decided to try."

Sharpe felt energized in his new academic career, frequently boasting of his long-term goal of helping mankind by finding the cure for cancer. His own parents were finally proud of their son's achievement, and he basked in their new-found pride in him.

Benjamin Sharpe told his son he was wasting his time on school, and should be satisfied working as a toolmaker, like he had. His brother Ben thought Richard was exploiting their parents by continually asking for money to fund his lofty academic aspirations.

"My father, by then, had become fairly mellow," said Ben Sharpe. "And I felt that Richard was now the aggressor and taking advantage."

But Richard had an ally in his mother, who dreamed of having a doctor in the family, and pressured her husband to give their son as much money as he could.

Shannon, now five years old, spent most of her time at the Hatfields' house, as her parents were always working. She started her schooling at their home, even having her own pet dog, Kiki, living there.

"We used to call it 'Camp Hatfield,'" remembered John Hatfield. "During the summers she was at our house most of the time."

Most days, Hatfield or one of his sons would collect little Shannon and drive her to Shelton, to spend the day with the family. But her grandmother Patricia would never let her go home at night until Karen was there.

"She wouldn't let [Shannon] leave if Richie was home alone," said Hatfield. "There was no molestation or anything like that. It was just that he was mean to her."

On birthdays and holidays Karen and Shannon were always there to help the family celebrate, but Richard rarely made an appearance, to the relief of everyone. When he did come to family gatherings, he'd deliberately turn up the volume on the record player, making himself the center of attention.

In the winter of 1978, the combined pressures of his master's and working a full-time job brought Sharpe near breaking point. Over the next several years he alienated his brothers in two particularly violent incidents, leading to deep rifts in the family.

On one occasion, Bob Sharpe hired his brother to help re-wire his new house in Milford. Karen arrived at midday, offering to bring them back some lunch, and Richard demanded a Whopper Meal from Burger King. When she returned with Kentucky Fried Chicken, as she couldn't find a Burger King, he went berserk.

"He took the whole bucket and threw it against my living room wall," remembered Bob. "It had just been painted and it took me two days to clean it and five paint jobs to fix it."

Robert fired his brother on the spot, telling him never to set foot in his house again.

Sharpe treated his wife like a possession, feeling he had every right to beat her at will. In August 1979 he actually hit her in front of a police officer, once again getting away with it.

It happened one evening after Karen had arrived back at their Hartford home to find him with another woman. An argument ensued, leading to the police being called.

"My husband hit me in the presence of an officer and he was arrested," Karen would later write. "The charges against him were subsequently dismissed."

On New Year's Eve 1980, his other brother Ben invited Richard and Karen to dinner at the Keg House Bar Restaurant in New Haven, Connecticut, which he had recently bought. Ben explained that he had to go to another party earlier in the evening, but promised to be there to toast the new year.

"My husband began drinking heavily early in the evening," Karen would remember. "[Then] he began verbally abusing not only me, but other individuals with whom we were celebrating the holiday."

When Ben arrived at the restaurant later that evening, his manager told him that Richard was obnoxiously drunk and upsetting the other patrons.

"I told him that he had to leave the restaurant," said Ben. "That he shouldn't come back anymore."

Sharpe stalked out in a rage, followed by an embarrassed Karen. Without saying a word, he got into his car, accelerated out of the parking lot and started jabbing his fist repeatedly into Karen's face.

"My husband relentlessly began hitting me and punching me," she would later remember. "Eventually we stopped at a hotel, but we were denied occupancy because I was covered in blood."

Sharpe then drove her to his cousin George's house to spend the night. He explained away his wife's battered and bloodied face by claiming she had gotten drunk and fallen down a flight of stairs, although Karen hadn't touched a drop of alcohol since high school.

"As a result of this incident, I suffered from a broken nose, a concussion, two black eyes and a split lip," she said.

Karen, who was later treated at Doctor's Hospital in New York, covered up the horrendous injuries she had suffered, wearing sunglasses and telling friends that she had fallen down stairs. Her life now began to follow a classic pattern of domestic abuse. She suffered in silence, unable to leave her tormentor. Already insecure when he had met her, Sharpe had systematically worn Karen down with his incessant humiliation and verbal and physical abuse. She now dreaded going out socially with him, never knowing what he would do next.

In the fall of 1980, Richard Sharpe got his master's degree and was accepted to medical school at the University of Connecticut in Farmington. Once again he moved Karen and Shannon to New Britain, forty miles away from her parents' house in Shelton. Now his dream of being a doctor became an obsession, and Karen and Shannon were ignored as he returned home from work to study into the early hours.

"I studied too hard," he later admitted. "I overachieved and I was in the top ninety percent of every test I took. I was afraid of failing."

Karen now became the sole breadwinner in the Sharpe household. To put him through medical school she worked two nursing jobs, and then came home to look after Shannon. Later, when he achieved success, he would never credit Karen's pivotal role in making it possible.

"Karen supported him," said her sister Kathleen. "He was constantly studying, and I mean constantly."

Sharpe also expected total quiet when he came home to study, and that Karen wait on him hand and foot.

At the end of his first year of medical school, Richard had ten weeks off between semesters. He volunteered to take part in a cancer research study, as well as finishing up a computer consultation project. Later he would claim that he and Karen had their best times in the early 1980s, when they were struggling to make ends meet.

"My happiest memories are when we sat down in the kitchen and counted the change in the bowl," he would later remember nostalgically. "And we would use it to go to the movies or something."

But their daughter Shannon remembered things very

differently. In a chilling sworn affidavit detailing the extreme abuse she and her mother suffered at the hands of her demented father, she described one particularly horrendous 1983 episode.

"When I was approximately ten years old, I recall an incident in which Richard threw acid in my mother's face," she would later remember. "I was invited to a slumber party that evening and my mother drove me to a friend's home early, so that I would not continue to witness this argument.

"During the evening, Richard traveled to my friend's house. I was terrified when I learned that he arrived because he never accompanied me or transported me anywhere during my childhood."

Shannon tried to hide in her friend's bathroom, but Sharpe burst in and dragged her out of the house, as the terrified little girl struggled desperately to escape.

"He threw me into his car, locking me in the backseat. And drove back and forth between Connecticut and Massachusetts."

They finally ended up at the home of one of her father's friends, whom she had never met. Sharpe then imprisoned his daughter in a second-floor bedroom, sleeping at the bottom of the stairs so she could not escape.

"He even insisted that I use the bathroom with the door open so I could not escape through the window," she said. "I cried all night for my mother, but he denied my repeated requests to contact her."

A few days later, while Karen was running errands, he forced Shannon to clear up a mess he had made at their home. When she refused to leave her bedroom he physically attacked her, repeatedly slamming her head against the wooden bedframe until she lost consciousness.

"My next memory is my head hitting the stairs as he dragged me down a flight of stairs, screaming and battering me. As a result of this incident, I suffered numerous abrasions and two black eyes. My mother kept me home from school for two days and upon my return, Richard instructed me to inform the school that I fell down a flight of stairs."

During her tortured childhood, Shannon witnessed countless acts of her father's violence against her and her mother. They found themselves trapped in a prison without any rules and no means of escape.

"[We were] fearful of the consequences if we fled," continued Shannon. "Through the years, Richard would threaten to kill not only us, but members of my mother's family, including her father and brothers, if my mother left him."

One Christmas in the early 1980s Sharpe decided to punish Karen, taking the keys to her car so she was stranded. She was forced to walk to work and became very depressed, not being able to do any Christmas shopping. When her father heard of her plight, he gave her one of his cars to use. Richard was furious, accusing his father-in-law of interfering in his life.

"They must have had a big battle," remembered John Hatfield, "and she left him."

Sharpe then called the local police to report the car stolen, in a vengeful attempt to have Karen arrested.

"I felt mad about it," said Karen's father. "I called the police to tell them it was not stolen and everything was OK."

Like the other occasions when she tried to leave during the first decade of their marriage, Sharpe managed to win her back with promises that he would change. But after they kissed and made up, he would soon revert back to his abusive ways.

Despite the intolerable conditions she lived under, Karen was always cheerful, with a smile on her face, so none of her friends guessed the terrible truth about her miserable, and increasingly dangerous, family life.

On the surface, the Sharpes seemed to be *the* perfect family, with everything going for them. It would be another twenty years before Karen would finally summon up the courage to walk out permanently.

In 1985 Richard Sharpe, at the age of thirty-one, received his medical degree and officially became a doctor. He seemed to be going places, renting a small house in Newton, Massachusetts, while he did a year-long postgraduate research fellowship at Massachusetts General Hospital. He then embarked on a three-year residency at the renowned Harvard Medical School.

Although his future seemed assured, the Sharpes were always in the red. During his residency, he was only making $17,000 a year, plus any extra money he made moonlighting on various computer-related projects. So Karen supplemented their income, working long hours in a nursing home.

"We couldn't make ends meet," recalled Sharpe. "We were living very spartan and just getting by."

In the first summer of his residency, according to Sharpe, they both had affairs; he with a classmate and she with a doctor where she worked.

". . . as usual, we kissed and made up," he said. "But actually things with Karen did get better when we got into a new life."

Over the next five years the Sharpes settled into a routine as Richard fulfilled the requirements of his Harvard residency. He also worked long hours on research experiments seven days a week, and much to Karen and Shannon's relief, he was hardly ever at home.

"It was really high-stress," he later remembered. "There were fewer verbal arguments and no physical fights. The time we had together was close, very high quality time."

But a friend of Shannon's recalls how Sharpe would often come home in the early hours, stinking of cheap perfume and alcohol, with lipstick smudges all over his starched white shirt.

"We all knew he was with another woman," said the friend.

While Karen loyally made excuses for her husband's deplorable behavior when he arrived home late, he would verbally assault her in front of Shannon's friends, screaming that she was a "bitch" and "fat" and "lazy," before skulking up to bed.

Despite all the stress she lived under, Karen became a substitute mother to many of her daughter's friends. She would drive them to the mall and the movies, afterwards inviting them back for chocolate cake.

"She was like an angel," said the friend, who felt sorry for Karen, because she always looked like she had been crying.

On Easter Sunday 1990, Karen's brother Jeff was hit by a car and killed in Florida. Although she was broken-hearted by his death, she immediately took care of all the arrangements, supporting her family through their grief.

"It was very hard on Karen," said her brother Jamie. "One of the vivid things I remember is that she was totally devastated, and she was also dealing with this monster at home."

Chapter Five

BREAKDOWN

In June 1990, Dr. Richard Sharpe completed his residency at Harvard Medical School, finding a job as a cancer research scientist with a biotech company at $50,000 a year. He continued part-time at Harvard in an academic teaching position, as well as joining the staff at Boston's Beth Israel Hospital.

To befit his new status as a doctor, he bought a condo at 170 Gore Street in Cambridge, and began looking for a country house around scenic Gloucester, Massachusetts. In order to finance his ambitious new lifestyle he studied to become a board certified dermatologist, taking over a part-time dermatology practice at the Cape Ann Medical Center in Gloucester, which had become vacant after the death of a physician.

Initially he only worked Saturday mornings, seeing patients between nine and two. But within a month demand for his services was so great, he added Sundays to his schedule. He was soon seeing patients seven days a week, with Karen working as his part-time receptionist and office manager.

"There was a lot of skin cancer in Gloucester," he

later explained. "A lot of people cooked themselves in the sun, and I started doing a lot of skin cancer surgery on patients."

But just three months after opening his practice, he was accused of killing a patient, whose widow sued him for malpractice.

"I felt angry," he said. "I didn't think I had done anything wrong."

Fearful of losing his license, Dr. Sharpe fell into a deep depression. He hardly ate, and was swallowing diet pills and steroids in an obsessive attempt to lose weight. He and Karen were also arguing about whether he should now give up research to concentrate solely on his thriving dermatology practice. Shannon, now a beautiful seventeen-year-old, was preparing to go to college where she could escape his tyranny and abuse. Stretching him even further, he began drafting a business plan with a friend named Dr. Maureen MacAloon, seeking venture capital for a new start-up medical company.

But the impending suit, which he would ultimately survive, and the eighty-hour weeks he was now working, did not stop him from embarking on a six-month love affair or passing his dermatology board exams in November.

In late 1990, Richard Sharpe bought a $300,000 house in West Gloucester at 8 Great Ledge Lane, in a secluded part of the town, inside two-and-a-half acres of woods across a narrow white bridge over a marsh. Their sprawling new house was at the far end of a cul-de-sac, with three other homes. The Sharpes had come a long way from blue-collar Shelton, and their new neighbors were affluent, well-to-do families.

Karen seemed energized, telling her new neighbor Carol Figurido that she had finally found her white picket fence. She took care of all the details, throwing herself into securing a mortgage and hiring builders for a major renovation.

For the next decade Richard Sharpe would make the historic whaling town his base, reaping millions of dollars from the various medical businesses he would hatch.

At the end of 1990, Richard was finding it so hard to function that his primary care physician suggested he go into therapy. So he began treatment with a Brookline psychiatrist named Dr. Margaret Ross, attending weekly sessions over the next year. Dr. Ross diagnosed him with "major depression with features of schizoid or other personality disorder," putting him on a course of the antidepressant Xanax.

"Basically I wasn't getting anything done," he would later explain. "I'd go to work and sit there and couldn't see patients for a month. But then after the medication kicked in, I started sleeping better and doing things."

But by April 1991 he was burnt out and his health was deteriorating. He became ill with gastroenteritis, suffering chronic dehydration and diarrhea. To make matters worse, he started drinking heavily and swallowing pills for relief.

On Friday, April 26, he was at the Gore Street condo and came into Shannon's bedroom, something he rarely did.

"[It] was highly unusual for him to pay attention to me," she would later explain in an affidavit. "He questioned what I was eating and I informed him it was Cool Whip."

Sharpe then left the room without another word.

Later that night, he went to his new house in Great Ledge Lane, to work on his new business plan. They still had not fully moved into the house, as it was still under renovation, and he felt ill and couldn't concentrate.

"The house seemed cold and empty," he would later remember. "I felt lonely."

After about half-an-hour he became physically sick, deciding to drive forty miles back to the Cambridge condo, where he felt more comfortable. But he walked in to discover Karen in bed with one of their male friends. Furious, Sharpe ordered the man to leave, and he and Karen had "a screaming contest," after Karen demanded a divorce.

Then he fell apart, telling her that "[I] would be better off dead" as "life was not worth living anymore," vowing to stand in the way of her ever getting a divorce. Indeed, he was so scared of losing Karen that he called Dr. Ross, who told him to take a sleeping pill and go to sleep.

He woke up early the next morning and the fight resumed, turning violent. Sharpe picked up a fork, stabbing Karen in the forehead several times, causing two deep lacerations. Fearing for her life, she kneed him in the groin and bit his hand, before fleeing from the house with Shannon.

They then drove to Great Ledge Lane where Karen called Dr. Ross, saying she was in terrible danger and asking for help. Concerned, the psychiatrist called Sharpe, finding him totally incoherent. Thinking he had overdosed, because of his slurred speech and total disorientation, she immediately called an ambulance. And when he finally regained consciousness on his way to Cambridge City Hospital, he tried to escape, but found himself strapped down.

Later in the emergency room, Sharpe was diagnosed as suffering from gastroenteritis and severe dehydration. He also had bite marks on his hand. After being given an IV and becoming coherent, he vehemently denied stabbing Karen with the fork, but was unable to account for her injuries, claiming not to remember what had happened.

Fearing he was a risk to himself and possibly violent, doctors transferred him to the Waltham–Weston Hospital and Medical Center (now the Deaconess Waltham Hospital). On arrival Dr. Sharpe underwent an extensive eight-hour psychiatric evaluation.

"[The] results revealed enough doubt that patient may represent a risk to his wife," wrote an examining doctor in his official report. "Karen Sharpe was also interviewed by doctors, telling them that her husband had often been violent in the past and how he had beaten her up ten years earlier on New Year's Eve. She also revealed that he had a problem with alcohol and had stopped drinking for two months prior to the stabbing. But a week earlier he had resumed and had been drinking 'to oblivion' ever since."

On Sunday at 5:20 p.m., Richard Sharpe was involuntary committed to the Arbour Hospital in Jamaica Plain, put in a strait jacket and placed in a locked ward for further evaluation.

"Psychiatric evaluation [of Dr. Sharpe] reveals much concern/doubt over violent homocidal [sic] behavior," read the pink slip application for his forcible commitment to the Arbour.

"This is a very difficult case with multiple contradictory data," reported the referring psychiatrist. "The final decision is made because of a desire to safeguard wife."

During the two days Dr. Sharpe was locked up in a secure psychiatric facility, Shannon became violently ill after eating Cool Whip, and had to be hospitalized.

"As soon as the Cool Whip touched my tongue, I observed a strong odor and the taste began to sting my tongue," she explained later in a sworn affidavit. "My next memory is the paramedics placing me on a couch and my subsequent hospitalization."

After Shannon was discharged from the hospital she returned home and made a frightening discovery.

"I observed syringe holes in my mother's diet bars," she said. "And I inhaled the same strong odor which I discovered in the Cool Whip. Even our dog's food was contaminated with the solution."

Ten years later Shannon would accuse her father in court papers of attempting to poison her with the Cool Whip the previous Friday. And she would claim he had utilized his medical knowledge to deliberately poison himself and be hospitalized with symptoms of gastroenteritis. She believed he had previously planned the stabbing attack on Karen, hoping to "dodge any responsibility" by making himself ill.

As Arbour Hospital doctors reviewed his medical records, learning of the childhood abuse by his father, his grandfather's suicide and the history of alcohol abuse in his family, Dr. Sharpe hired an attorney named Christopher Nolan to get himself released. Scared that his involuntary commitment to a locked psychiatric facility, and his ferocious attack on Karen, could jeopardize his medical license, he told Karen he would kill her father unless she and Shannon recanted their allegations.

"Richard was concerned about 'these blemishes on his record,'" Shannon wrote, adding that he also threatened to stop paying her college tuition. "He continually terrorized my mother and me [and] suggested that something terrible would happen to [us] if my cooperation was not forthcoming. I was led to believe that I would either be killed or left starving in the streets. I was terrified by the possibilities that would ensue if I did not adhere to his demands."

On Monday morning Karen arrived at Arbour Hospital and retracted her earlier statements. In a handwritten letter, she now claimed to have made up the stabbing incident, apologizing for the "trouble" her "stories" had created. She now presented a revisionist view of events the previous Friday night:

> I would like to retract all negative comments that I made about my husband. The true story is that: He came home at 11:00 p.m. on Friday night to find me with another man in our Cambridge apartment. He became upset and told the other man to leave. He & I argued all night long. I was asking him for a divorce. He was throwing up and having diarrhea during this time. At 4:00 a.m. he called Dr. Margaret Ross to ask to meet with us that day to try to help salvage our marriage. Dr. Ross agreed but I refused.
>
> At 8:00 a.m. I was getting ready to leave Rich and take my belongings. He was begging me not to go. He said he loved me & for me to please stay. He wanted to hug me. I pushed him away and left the condominium. I started to try and think of a way to get a divorce from him so I could be with the other man and that was when I started to make the phone calls that I made thinking that I would make him mad and then he would agree to the divorce.
>
> Richard is not violent and has never tried to hurt me or hurt himself. The stories that I told were untrue.
>
> Signed: Karen Sharpe

A day earlier, under penalty of perjury, Dr. Sharpe had written his own version of events, claiming: "at no time did I physically assault my wife." He maintained that the only psychiatric problems he had ever experienced were "some mild situational anxiety/depression," for which he had been treated by his psychiatrist.

"My wife made some untrue statements concerning my physical abuse of her," he maintained. "My medical opinion is that my transient confusional state during the morning of April 27th was due to a lack of sleep, severe dehydration secondary to gastroenteritis and the drug Xanax. This metabolic (and not emotional) confusion has completely resolved."

Saying he realized he had marital difficulties, he denied ever wanting to harm his wife, her boyfriend or himself.

"I have a dual career as a physician and a scientist which I would like my freedom to pursue in an unobstructed fashion," he wrote.

A few hours after receiving Karen's revised statement, the hospital had no alternative but to release Dr. Sharpe, declaring him "non-psychotic."

But that wasn't the end of it. Accusing doctors of treating him "like a dangerous lunatic," Sharpe then sued the Arbour Hospital, the city of Cambridge, the Waltham–Weston Hospital, as well as his health insurance company, to expunge all mention of the stabbing incident from his medical records.

For the next three years he and his attorney Christopher Nolan fought to erase what he termed a "false and extremely embarrassing medical record." A judge finally ruled against him in 1994, but sealed the records, allowing him to insert his own written explanation of what had occurred.

It would be another six years before the records would be made public. But by then, it would be too late to save Karen Sharpe.

Chapter Six

MIKEY AND ALI

After Dr. Sharpe's discharge from the Arbour Hospital, a heavily bandaged Karen drove him back to the Cambridge condo and cooked him his favorite meal of baked lasagna and salad. According to Sharpe, they were both in shock from the violent fight two days earlier, and spent the next several days making passionate love.

"I think we were both confused," Sharpe would later remember. "It was a blur."

Over the next two months Sharpe spent most of his time in Cambridge while Karen moved into 8 Great Ledge Lane, to supervise renovations. She also found a job at a nearby Cape Ann nursing home named Greycliffs, in addition to helping her husband in his new dermatology practice.

But incredibly, despite the ferocity of his attack on his wife, the doctor felt no remorse.

"I was concerned that she wanted me back, not because she loved me, but because I was a meal ticket," said Sharpe. "I didn't know whether or not we could stay together."

Karen never told anyone about her husband's brief

committal to a locked psychiatric hospital ward.

"She told us that he had tried to commit suicide," said her sister Kathleen. "I didn't know all of the details because she wouldn't give us them."

So for the next nine years, only Karen and Shannon knew just how dangerous Richard could be. Feeling trapped in an almost surrealistic world ruled by a "terrorist," Shannon's frustrations often expressed themselves as anger at her mother. But whenever she demanded to know why Karen stayed with "this monster," she later told a magazine reporter, the reply was always that she was terrified he would carry out his threat to kill their whole family.

In spite of everything she'd been through during the eighteen years of their marriage, Karen still loved him. She genuinely hoped one day he would revert back to the high school sweetheart she had fallen in love with. Against all odds, she believed his extravagant promises to give up drinking and drugs and change his life for the better. Like so many women trapped in the vortex of battered women's syndrome, the combination of fear and hope was an extremely powerful one for Karen.

After his release Richard begged forgiveness, promising Karen a new life in Gloucester, and that everything would be different. He also hatched a devious plan to ensure that Karen never tried to leave him again. He encouraged her to stop using birth control, saying she was too old to become pregnant.

Dr. Sharpe continued his sessions with Dr. Ross until July 1991, and then stopped going. He blamed the psychiatrist for having him committed and now decided to handle his own treatment, medicating himself for anxiety and depression.

"Actually I was fairly cheap," he would later explain.

"What I'd do was to ask the doctors' nurses at the medical center for samples so I could treat myself with either Prozac, Zoloft or whatever drugs I could get for free."

Now back together, Karen and Richard moved permanently to Great Ledge Lane, renting out their Cambridge condo as well as an apartment over the garage in their new home. He also bought a brand new black Porsche 911, one of many he would own over the next few years. Neighbors would soon get used to the noise of Sharpe, gunning the Porsche around the back roads of Gloucester late at night.

Although the Sharpes now had all the trappings of success, the doctor's behavior became even more erratic, as he numbed himself with prescription pills and glass after glass of his favorite merlot.

Attending a family get-together in Gloucester that October, Sharpe started drinking before Karen's family even arrived at the restaurant. As usual there was tension during the meal, as the Hatfields negotiated the predictable minefield around Richard Sharpe. This time they had hoped things might be different. A few months earlier Karen had called her sister Kathleen, saying he had promised to quit drinking, so he wouldn't "act up" anymore. But that night it was obvious to everyone that he was back on the red wine with a vengeance.

Sharpe left the restaurant early and went home by himself. A couple of hours later Karen drove her parents, sister Kathleen and brother Jamie back to Great Ledge Lane. As she came up the driveway, she saw her husband standing naked at a window, and froze, asking: "What's he doing now?"

Telling her family to wait in the car, she went inside to find him parading around the house naked, after coming out of his hot tub. She ordered him to go back upstairs to put on some clothes, as her family were sleeping over that night. Going back out, she told everyone it was now safe to come in.

For the next hour there was no sign of Dr. Sharpe, much to the relief of Karen's family. But suddenly he came downstairs, walked into the living room and without saying a word punched Karen's big bear of a brother, Jamie, hard in the stomach.

"What are you doing?" shouted Karen in astonished embarrassment.

"I was just fooling around. I didn't mean it," replied her husband, trying to defuse the situation.

Then six-foot, three-inch Jamie, who weighed 240 pounds, stood up to physically confront his weedy, drunken brother-in-law, who was seven inches shorter.

"Jamie wanted to push him through a window," said Kathleen. "We also talked briefly about calling the police."

Patricia Hatfield was particularly upset by her son-in-law's behavior, pleading with Jamie not to hit him, as Sharpe laughed it off as a joke.

"I told Karen that we've got to get out of here because he'd had too much to drink," said Jamie. "My mom and everyone were very upset. I think in his own demented mind he was being territorial, and trying to make us and Karen feel uncomfortable."

Kathleen, who was pregnant at the time, urged Karen to call the police and spend the night in a hotel. But she refused, saying she had to calm him down. On the way out the door Kathleen looked Richard straight in the eyes, warning him *never* to hit Karen. Again he shrugged off the whole episode, saying he was being playful and just fooling around. But no one had the slightest doubt it was entirely deliberate.

After that Kathleen and her clergyman husband, Victor Lembo, told Karen they would not be attending any family gatherings if Richard was invited.

"It became a family issue," said Kathleen. "That Thanksgiving my father said [Richard] had to be invited to our house, otherwise Karen's not going to come with Shannon. I said that would have to be her decision."

But by Christmas the Lembos had decided to bite the bullet for Karen's sake, and a victorious Richard attended the family's seasonal festivities as if nothing had ever happened.

In the fall of 1991 Dr. Sharpe and his partner Dr. Maureen MacAloon raised $600,000 to start a new medical company, which they christened the Arcturus Pharmaceutical Corporation. Sharpe appointed himself CEO of the start-up company, quitting his research job at the biotech corporation to run it.

The new high-tech company developed products for skin disorders, such as psoriasis. Over the next few years Dr. Sharpe helped develop and bring to market several medical products which were awarded four patents, with a dozen more in the pipeline.

He was now devoting more and more time to his own dermatological practice at Cape Ann Medical Center, even giving free cancer screenings for patients who couldn't afford to go elsewhere. While working at the medical center, he became friends with an internist named Dr. Cynthia Bjorlie, who owned part of the building and was his landlord.

"He was an odd guy," she would later remember. "I thought his personality was a little dysfunctional."

Initially the two doctors referred patients back and forth, but Dr. Bjorlie soon began to get negative feedback from various patients about Sharpe's unorthodox medical procedures. They complained that he made them strip naked before any examination, however cursory, and of being kept waiting for hours.

And Dr. Bjorlie also saw how he treated Karen, when she came into the office to help him.

"Sharpe would yell at his wife until people were extremely uncomfortable about it," she said.

Nevertheless, many patients considered him a great doctor and highly professional. And positive word of mouth grew his practice over the next few years, as he gained an international reputation among his peers for numerous published articles in the medical journals on subjects like topical immunosuppressants.

By now he was affiliated with the Beth Israel Deaconess Medical Center and the Beverly and Addison Gilbert Hospitals, as well as regularly teaching at Harvard Medical School. But he always walked a tightrope between greatness and disaster. And his escalating use of prescription pills, combined with alcohol, would make him increasingly erratic and unstable.

At the beginning of 1992 Karen became pregnant at the age of thirty-six. She was ecstatic. Eighteen years after Shannon's birth she prepared for a new baby, contemplating a wonderful new future as a mother. Karen told Kathleen that she had stopped using birth control, thinking she could no longer have children, and had been completely taken by surprise when she became pregnant.

Karen's family were secretly horrified when she told them, fearful that Sharpe had merely built a new prison she could never escape from.

"We were devastated," said Kathleen, who had recently given birth to a daughter, Katie. "She had gotten to the point where she could have left him, as Shannon was almost an adult. I thought that this was yet another means to control her. But she was thrilled."

Michael Richard Sharpe was born on September 22, 1992, in Gloucester, and was a beautiful healthy baby boy. Dr. Sharpe was there at the delivery, giving advice to the nursing staff, citing his vast medical experience.

"She was ecstatic after Michael was born," said Karen's friend Linda Stockman. "She loved motherhood. It was the focus of her life."

And for a short time things were better in the Sharpe household, as Richard played the part of the doting father. Later he would claim to have been uncertain whether the marriage would survive until Michael's birth, claiming that it had been Karen who had talked him into giving it another chance.

Immediately after the birth, Karen told her sister she wanted another child, so Michael wouldn't have to grow up alone like Shannon. From then on she stopped talking about divorce, as she began a new life devoted to motherhood.

Since the move to Gloucester, Karen had been feeling far more independent and enjoying more freedom, as Richard was always working. But whenever she went to visit Kathleen in Connecticut, he would continually be calling to check up on her.

"If she was down here he would call two or three times," remembered Kathleen. "When the phone would ring, she'd say, 'That's Richie. He's checking up on me.'"

In his later glossed-over version of his marriage, Dr. Sharpe would describe the idyllic existence he and Karen shared after Michael's birth. However "bad" his day had been, he would return to Great Ledge Lane and start "hugging and playing" with his new baby.

"Karen and I grew closer than we had ever been," he would write. "We wanted more children."

On November 17, 1995, Karen gave birth to a daughter they christened Alexandra Elizabeth. Once again Dr. Sharpe was in the delivery room, torn between being the dutiful father and playing doctor.

"[I] helped with the delivery and scooped Ali away from the nurse and suctioned her tiny mouth," he explained. "I thought the nurse was moving too slowly [so I] administered oxygen."

Hours after she was born, little Ali developed a fever and had to be treated with drugs for suspected B-strep sepsis throat infection, before being allowed to go home. The next day the little baby became "lethargic," with her father "suspecting the worst." He met with her doctor, who wanted to treat the baby in a children's hospital.

"I refused, since that would further delay things," said Dr. Sharpe.

Taking matters into his own hands, Sharpe treated his new baby himself, taking blood cultures from a lumbar puncture. Then Ali was admitted to the hospital, where Sharpe noted "two medical errors." He feared a nurse had wrongly diluted an antibiotic with a normal saline solution, as well as giving Ali the wrong dosage. But he held his tongue as the little girl was discharged home into his care.

"Instead of arguing, I treated Ali with an additional seven days of Rocephin," he would later write. "I took about two weeks off work and spent almost every minute with Ali."

Ali fully recovered under his care, becoming an object of "curiosity and confusion," for her three-year-old brother Michael, now nicknamed "Mikey."

"He soon grew to love Ali as much as Karen and I," said Dr. Sharpe. But everyone else would wonder why Mikey would try at all costs to avoid his father and seemed to hate him.

Chapter Seven

MAKING MONEY

While Karen was pregnant with Ali, Richard Sharpe and
Maureen MacAloon started a new high-tech private corporation called Clickmed. Flushed with the success of
Arcturus, which had successfully developed the highly
lucrative line of Alpha Hydroxy Gold skin rejuvenation
products, Sharpe wrote a sophisticated computer program called "Women's HealthTrack." The software was
designed to help physicians track mammogram and pap
smear results on a database, and could also be net-
worked. A second program of his, Clickmed Medical
Practice software, aided health professionals with billing
and patient administration.

Headquartered in an office at Great Ledge Lane,
Sharpe hired a receptionist named Rose Horne, then recruited a patient of his named Suzanne Crossen as the
new company's chief financial officer and bookkeeper
for his private practice. The attractive mother of two
would be the first of a long line of patients he would
hire in various capacities over the years.

When Crossen first went to Dr. Sharpe's practice, he
had told her to strip naked for a full body exam. He

found a mole on her lower back, which he removed.

"He asked what I did," remembered Crossen. "I told him that I had just had a new baby and had given up a career in banking. I was looking for some part-time work."

Sharpe offered her a job on the spot and she accepted, considering it a good opportunity. But within a few weeks she had discovered that her new boss had a terrible temper and completely lacked social skills.

"He's a horrible person," she would later say. "Just about as miserable a person that you can imagine."

During her six years working for Dr. Sharpe, he would often swear at her, calling her "a fucking asshole" and a "bitch."

"He would use profanities when he was frustrated," she said. "He just didn't treat me very nicely [with] common courtesies or just regular manners that we expect nowadays in business."

Crossen was also shocked by the coldness towards Karen and their two young children, whenever they came to the office. He would swear and belittle her in front of his staff, and ignore Mikey and Ali. She also thought it strange that the married couple lived such parallel lives, hardly ever interacting.

But despite his unorthodox attitude towards business, Clickmed and his private practice flourished, making big money. He started investing in the soaring stock market of the late 1990s, and would make a fortune out of tech stocks on the NASDAQ.

Soon after moving to Gloucester, Karen Sharpe began making her own set of friends. In 1993 she met a young mother named Connie Behnke, while working out at the Manchester Athletic Club. The two women, both in their thirties, found much in common, having both come from rural farming communities in the Midwest.

"There was a connection," explained Behnke, who lived three miles away from Karen in Essex. "We could laugh about the North Shore elite together. We started going out to lunch and to the beach with the kids. My husband Jim travels all the time, so we were two women home alone with little kids, supporting each other."

Two years into their friendship, Connie and Jim Behnke first met Richard Sharpe, after Karen arranged a dinner at an Italian restaurant in Beverly. And although Karen had carefully prepared her friend, saying Richard was "anti-social" and "not always nice," she was still shocked by his odd behavior.

"It was really awful," she remembered. "I thought he was *so* bizarre."

Sharpe dominated the conversation through dinner, talking business and making blatant pitches for Jim Behnke to invest in Clickmed. Whenever Karen tried to steer the conversation onto other things, her husband would angrily berate her for being "stupid," "ugly" and "fat."

"He didn't value Karen's intellect or anything about her," said Connie. "If she started to say anything he'd just say, 'Oh, shut up. You don't know what you're talking about.' We were excruciatingly sympathetic, but there was nothing we could do. It was really unpleasant."

That summer Shannon accompanied her father to Paris for a business conference. One night when he was drinking, Shannon later told a friend, he started inviting strangers in the bar to dance with her. Now a beautiful twenty-one-year-old woman, Shannon's model looks always turned heads. But to many observers there was something unnatural about how her father treated her.

Shannon would later tell this friend how uncomfortable her father's behavior had made her in Paris.

"I thought it was kind of weird," said the friend. "I

wouldn't want some guy doing it to my daughter."

Although she was now in college, Shannon spent most of her spare time at Great Ledge Lane, playing with Mikey and Ali, whom she adored. As the money started rolling in, Richard tried to control his daughter, offering her highly paid but undemanding sales jobs for his companies.

Now highly visible in the world of dermatology, Dr. Sharpe's well-received articles for trade magazines established him as an expert in his field. He and Karen attended many dermatological trade shows and conferences around the country, setting up the Clickmed booth and courting new customers.

At one trade fair a few years earlier he had even dressed up in full drag, eagerly posing for Karen to take pictures. With his long flowing black wig, heavy make-up, fishnet stockings and plunging red blouse, he seemed to favor the sluttish look.

To make himself even more feminine he had recently had all his body hair removed, except from his head, as well as undergoing numerous plastic surgeries on his nose and eyes, and removing surplus fat with liposuction.

"I didn't like hair," he would later explain. "And the other advantage was if I cross-dressed."

Years later Karen's pictures of him in full drag would come back to haunt him, when they were made public and caused a sensation.

Although Karen tolerated her husband's cross-dressing, she was shocked when she discovered he was again stealing her birth control pills to enlarge his breasts, and had taken to wearing her and Shannon's lingerie.

"My husband began taking prescription medicines, including female hormones with great frequency," Karen would later explain in a sworn affidavit. "He would often arrive home intoxicated, incoherent and his speech would be slurred."

Shannon Sharpe had first learned of her father's strange attraction to women's clothes while in grade school, and was "confused, bewildered and embarrassed."

"He would habitually steal my underwear, as well as my mother's, from our bureaus," she would later testify. "Richard is a cross-dresser and has been active in the trans-gender community."

One night in 1995, he was stopped by police in his Porsche on his way home, while stoned on a cocktail of prescription medicines, and charged with reckless driving. He hired a lawyer to defend him and once again managed to hush it up and keep his medical license.

"I sincerely believe that my husband has a dependency on prescription medicines which affects his ability to function emotionally, physically and socially on a daily basis," Karen later wrote.

And the doctor was also addicted to obsessively working out. After work he'd go to the gym six nights a week for what he called "stress relief," wearing tight spandex pants over his Victoria's Secret panties.

Although the rest of the world thought him strange, Richard Sharpe viewed himself as the quintessential family man. Years later he would remember the period after Ali was born as the happiest of his life. He endlessly reminisced about being the perfect father to anyone who would listen.

"I mean, even though I was still a workaholic, I thought it was great," he remembered. "When Ali was a baby we would bring her to the big waterbed and she'd sleep between us. And Mikey would climb in bed with us too. I was happy with the kids."

· · ·

In late 1996, Karen enrolled four-year-old Mikey in pre-school at the Shannah Montessori School, near their home in Gloucester. She accidentally discovered the tiny shop-front school one day, while walking down Hesperus Avenue by the harbor. It would transform her life.

"She was just waving in the window," said headmistress Karen Beswick, who had started the school a few months earlier, with only twenty pupils, "and being the sort of person she was, she came straight in."

Over the next three years, Karen enthusiastically devoted herself to the school. She persuaded Connie Behnke to send her two young children there, and the two mothers would meet every day, as they car-pooled to school and back.

The Shannah school soon became the hub of Karen's day; a means of escaping her unhappiness at home, and feeling appreciated.

"She was very bubbly," said Beswick, who soon became close friends with Karen. "She would come through the door and straightaway, your problems were solved. She was a big part of our day, and sometimes I'd just have to kick her out, because she just wanted to stay."

Most mornings, a smiling Karen would arrive laden with chocolate and cakes for the children, before running out to buy cups of coffee for teachers. And she generously paid for a series of colorful classroom murals and a large tank full of exotic fish.

Karen's happy-go-lucky personality endeared her to everyone. But although she involved herself in everyone else's lives, she rarely discussed her own.

On Michael's fifth birthday, Karen invited the whole school to a party at Great Ledge Lane. It was a joyous occasion, but Beswick noted that the little boy's dad was nowhere to be seen. She had already met Dr. Sharpe a couple of times, when he picked up Mikey from school, and was astonished that Karen could be married to such a cold, anti-social man.

"I would have to say that my first impression [of Richard] was that he was a very odd man," said Beswick. "But after I became friends with Karen I thought, How dare I think that?"

In early 1998, two-year-old Ali joined the toddlers' class at the school, as Michael moved on to kindergarten. Karen was now becoming more and more involved in the social life of the school. She enthusiastically helped to organize Christmas shows, Mother's and Father's Day tea parties and end-of-the-year graduation ceremonies. But Richard Sharpe rarely attended any of these, and when he did, he deliberately humiliated Karen.

"He showed up in a fancy woman's blouse at one of our school concerts," said Beswick. "Karen was horrified." Throughout the evening the other parents whispered about his bizarre appearance, but Dr. Sharpe acted as if everything was normal.

"I was so upset for Karen," said the headmistress. "She was very composed, but I could see it in her face. It was like he went out of his way to make a show of himself and embarrass her."

On another intimate parent evening, he spent most of his time on his cell phone doing business, making all the other parents and children highly uncomfortable.

"It was very rude, inappropriate behavior," said Beswick, noting that Mikey was "glued" to Karen and avoided his dad. And when she asked Mikey to show his father some crafts he had made, the little boy refused, shouting, 'I'm not showing him!' "

His headmistress was so concerned about Mikey's apparent hostility to his father, she called Karen into her office to discuss it.

"Karen made it OK for me in my mind," she said. "She kind of smoothed it over and made me take a step back and say, 'I'm overreacting.'"

Connie Behnke was also concerned about Mikey's almost "unnatural" attachment to his mother. The little boy hated to be parted from Karen. He often refused to go to school and summer camp, never wanting to leave his home for outside play dates. Slowly, as Karen began to confide in dribs and drabs the abuse she suffered, Behnke realized that Mikey was actually trying to *protect* his mother from his father.

"He was worried about her," said Connie. "He didn't want to be away from her, and when he was, he wanted to call her constantly."

Behnke believes that, as the older child, Mikey was far more attuned to the horrors he witnessed at home than his younger sister was.

"He was a really sad little boy," she said. "He picked up a lot more than Ali."

Living at home, Shannon Sharpe had the best vantage point to view her father's relationship with Mikey and Ali. Later she would accuse him of "ignoring" the two young children since birth, never making "any effort" to have a relationship with them.

"My siblings have endured a lifetime of grief and sorrow," she would explain in a subsequent custody proceeding.

Chapter Eight

THE MILLIONAIRE

By July 1997, Dr. Richard Sharpe had made his first million dollars, mainly from clever investments in the stock market. Over the past couple of years he had successfully ridden the gravy train on the dramatic success of tech stocks, buying heavily in Microsoft and Dell.

"In 1993 our net worth was zero," he would proudly explain. "In 1997 we probably had a million dollars."

In order to create a tax shelter for his new fortune, he set up irrevocable educational trusts for Mikey and Ali. He placed $50,000 in each of them, with similar amounts to be put in annually, appointing his friend Maureen MacAloon as the trustee.

Later he would maintain that his reasons were entirely selfless, saying he wanted to provide for his two young children's education. But many would question his true motives in setting up the complicated trusts with a leading tax attorney.

"I felt very strongly that I needed to protect my children with respect to their education, so they wouldn't work nonstop like Karen and I had to," he would claim.

"Maureen knew my investment strategy and the money grew fairly quickly."

Throughout their marriage, Dr. Sharpe was careful to put all property and investments in his name alone, so Karen had no money of her own and was fully dependent on him. She had absolutely no idea he was now a millionaire, as he never discussed business with her.

Nevertheless, he delighted in boasting to his staff about his success in the stock market and his savvy business acumen. And although he didn't live like a wealthy man, wearing shoes with holes in them and never taking his family on vacation, he bought and sold expensive sports cars on impulse.

One day Karen excitedly called Connie Behnke, saying that Richard had promised to take her and the children for a short break to White Plains, New York. She was delighted about the trip, as Richard had promised that the family would finally have a real holiday together.

"Well, it turned out that he had scheduled some liposuction for himself at a clinic and needed someone to drive him there," remembered Connie. "So many times she'd come back after being so hopeful and there would be another awful story."

But if any of her friends ever dared criticize her husband, Karen would leap to his defense and take his side against them.

"It's that classic, you've got to listen and offer advice, but be very careful not to go too far," said Behnke. "If you haven't been through that, it's hard to understand how someone can live with it."

One time Karen heard that friend and neighbor Carol Figurido had said something derogatory about Richard, and refused to talk to her for several months.

"She was really defensive," Figurido told *Boston*

Magazine. "She always made excuses for him."

One night during a blizzard, Figurido witnessed Richard crashing his Porsche into the back of a snow plow. As she watched in astonishment he calmly walked away from the scene, leaving Karen, Mikey and Ali to venture out in the below-zero conditions to get for help.

Christmas was particularly difficult for Karen. From early childhood, Dr. Sharpe had an almost pathological hatred of the season, when his moods would become darker than ever. Every year was the same. He'd get depressed and drink to excess over the holiday period, becoming more and more abusive and unpredictable. Towards the end of their marriage, Karen stopped inviting her family over for Christmas Day, waiting until a week later when he'd calmed down a bit.

"Christmas was horrible for her," said Behnke. "There were certain times when she knew he was going to drink heavily and be really nasty. Christmas was one of them. There was something about that holiday that he hated, and she worried about it a lot."

Connie so hated to see her best friend in the kitchen the entire Christmas Day, cooking for just Richard and the children, that she and her husband Jim, who disliked the doctor, made a point of joining them for dinner, just for Karen's sake.

"Richard was better behaved when somebody else was there," she explained. "And I felt, Here's this incredible woman and we're the only thing that's going to make her Christmas. We were trying to neutralize things a little bit."

During this period, the two friends started going for long five-mile walks around scenic Gloucester, and Karen began to confide that she was trapped in an abusive marriage. She started telling her story a piece at a time, until Connie realized just how bad things were.

"If she hadn't told it in little bits I don't know how I would have reacted," said Behnke. "It started in certain ways when she was really young and as he ratcheted it up, she got used to it and could deal with it."

But even then, Karen didn't mention the 1991 fork-stabbing incident, saying there were a couple of episodes she couldn't discuss, as they were "too out there."

Dr. Sharpe's practice and businesses were a revolving door of nurses and administrative staff, due to his anti-social behavior. He had recently left the Cape Ann Medical Center to start a new practice on Mill Pond Road in Gloucester, but his temper tantrums and abuse caused many of his staff to walk out in disgust.

Karen did her best to try to calm things down, making excuses for her husband's bad manners. Without her pacifying influence, his businesses might never have gotten off the ground.

One day Dr. Sharpe got angry over some medical bills, unleashing a tirade of profanities at his bookkeeper Suzanne Crossen, who promptly burst into tears and resigned. She stormed out of the office, having to be comforted by a nurse before she could go home.

A few hours later she received a telephone call from Karen, begging her to rescind her resignation.

"She asked me what it would take for me to stay," remembered Crossen. "I said I'd had it with him and I just couldn't put up with it anymore."

Karen Sharpe then suggested an arrangement where Crossen would no longer have to deal with Richard. She offered to personally deliver all her work to her home and then collect it.

"He never would have made a cent without her," said Connie Behnke. "He may have been the big Harvard guy, but he had no people skills. It was like she was the manager and he never would have survived without her on the sidelines to make it work."

In 1997 he hired an attractive blonde in her thirties, named Jacqueline Feeney, to be his new technician and medical assistant, after the previous one walked out. At the time, Jacqui, a patient of Dr. Sharpe's, was working as a waitress in the Halibut Point restaurant in downtown Gloucester, when a friend told her she was quitting her job and there was an opening.

She went for an interview and was immediately accepted for the job, which only paid $10 an hour. She was then given a crash course in testing biopsy slides under the microscope for melanoma.

"I was interested because I wanted to get into the medical field," said Feeney. "I started working on my own during the very first week."

Initially, Feeney took a dislike to the "creepy-looking" doctor, but soon grew to respect him for his "commitment" to cancer treatment.

"He was a bully and very short with women," she said. "He was always rushing around, screaming and yelling. He would go off over really small things, but that would blow over just as quickly."

The first time her new boss yelled at her was over a Sharpie, furious that she didn't know it was an ink pen.

"He blew up," she remembered. "I just told him I didn't respect anybody that yells at a woman."

Sharpe backed down and there was an uneasy truce between them for a couple of weeks. But then he exploded at her again in front of a patient.

"I went, 'Stop!' and started slamming things around," she said. "After that he treated me completely differently. We became friends."

But the other members of his staff, like his long-suffering receptionist Rose Horne and nurse Ellen Flaherty, never stood up for themselves and were constantly bullied.

In May 1999, Dr. Sharpe was profiled in an Associated Press health story about new breakthroughs in dermatology. He was delighted, proudly showing off the syndicated feature around the office and adding it to his growing press kit.

That July, Dr. Sharpe was on his best behavior when his childhood friend Frank Pelaggi came to Gloucester with his girlfriend for an extended weekend. Karen, who had known Pelaggi at Shelton High School, planned the trip. She booked them into the Cape Ann Marina, a short ride from Great Ledge Lane, and organized a whale watch.

Pelaggi would later remember the time he spent with the Sharpes fondly, saying Richard treated his wife well, and that he never saw any signs of abuse during the time they all spent together.

But a month later he was as difficult as ever, showing little interest when Karen single-handedly organized a Shelton High School reunion. It was a big deal to Karen and she enthusiastically tracked down all their old school friends, sending them invitations. She booked a venue for a party, planned a dinner menu and even arranged for everyone to stay at a hotel in Shelton.

"She was fanatical about what she was going to wear," remembered Behnke. "She wanted to go back and have people say, 'Gee, you look great.' "

But all hopes for a perfect night with her old crowd were dashed when Richard took Xanax and muscle relaxants, downing glass after glass of wine. Then he became jealous when he thought Karen was flirting with an old boyfriend, after she requested a particular song.

"He threw a glass of wine at the disk jockey," Karen later said. "The police arrived."

Once again the doctor wriggled out of trouble by giving the DJ a thousand dollars in return for not pressing charges. Karen was devastated by this humiliation in front of her old friends, whom she'd so wanted to impress.

On her return to Gloucester, she locked herself away in her basement for three days and nights. She pulled all the blinds shut, refusing to return any of her friends' calls.

"That was the only time she couldn't climb out of it," remembered Connie Behnke. "She was crying and her eyes were so puffed up as she told me the story about what had happened with the police. I'd never seen her like that. I think that to push her around at that point would be nothing compared to embarrassing her in front of the friends they had gone to high school with. He had really figured out how to hurt her."

Chapter Nine

LASEHAIR

In summer 1998, Dr. Richard Sharpe decided there wasn't enough money in treating cancer, devoting himself full-time to more lucrative laser hair removal and cosmetic surgery. His one-time dream of finding a cure for cancer had long been forgotten, as he now looked to make a financial killing in the burgeoning American beauty industry.

"It all happened very quickly," said Jacqui Feeney, who assisted him in the new project. "He just got online and started e-mailing people who did electrolysis. Then they'd come in and he'd explain how they could make more money working for him, offering them a percentage. In the course of a couple of months he had sixteen sites in Massachusetts, and then he started going further afield."

Dr. Sharpe bought a mobile laser and at least four permanent lasers from the Wayland, Massachusetts, firm of Candela Corporation, and installed them in selected affiliates. He also purchased a battered old sky-blue Ford handicapped van complete with ramp, to load and unload the heavy equipment. He starting teaching Jacqui how to operate the laser, which he had first worked with at medical school. With minimum training, she began accompanying him on extended trips to his affiliates dotted around the state, where they'd treat patients.

"He tried to pay me nothing," said the former waitress. "I said, 'You look at me like that van. I'm a bargain.'"

Eventually, he grudgingly agreed to pay her ten percent of his earnings for each trip, which could be as much as $10,000, depending on the number of patients he treated.

The first overnight trip they took together was to open up a new site at a Hyannisport gym, which he had rented for a weekend every month. Karen and her two young children went along for the ride, and Jacqui observed the Sharpe family outside the business for the first time.

"They didn't fight or anything," she said. "But I never saw any affection either. And they never touched each other." During the two-day trip, Feeney noticed that Mikey seemed rather distant from his father and uncomfortable in his presence.

Dr. Sharpe had a price list for all his treatments, which included liposuction, hair removal, collagen treatments, power peel, face lifts and Botox. Ironically, although he was in the process of growing his own breasts with Karen's birth control pills, he was totally opposed to surgical breast enhancement, refusing to perform the operation.

For the first few months business was brisk. Feeney often worked twelve-hour days and felt she and Dr. Sharpe made a good team. Often, after a busy day treating patients in his practice, Dr. Sharpe would invite her for dinner at Legal Sea Foods, his favorite restaurant in nearby Peabody. Invariably he would start drinking merlot wine, getting drunk and boasting how women found him irresistible. Occasionally he seemed drowsy, sometimes falling asleep in the middle of a meal. Later Jacqui would find out that he was secretly swallowing an assortment of prescription drugs.

That fall, business began to slow down, and Dr. Sharpe hired his daughter Shannon, who had been living in Arizona, to come and work for him. He put her on a $100,000-a-year salary to help him grow his cosmetic empire and find new business. Now twenty-five years old, Shannon threw herself into the work, hitting the phones and cold-calling prospective new partners. She had soon opened up fresh sites all over the Boston area and as far away as Concord.

As the money began flowing in, Dr. Sharpe moved his practice to Cape Ann Market Place, Gloucester, and constructed a new office over the garage at Great Ledge Lane. A young carpenter named Desi Smith, who also moonlighted as a photographer for the *Gloucester Daily Times*, worked on the project for three weeks, getting to know Karen and Richard Sharpe well.

"A lot of people say he's a jerk," remembered Smith, "but he was very sociable with me."

Every day, Smith would arrive at Great Ledge Lane to be greeted by a smiling Karen, asking him if he wanted a cup of tea. Then after a morning laying cables for Dr. Sharpe's new state-of-the-art telephone and computer system, she'd invite him to join her for lunch, with little Mikey and Ali.

"She was always smiling," said Smith. "You could tell she was a really caring mother just from the way she dealt with the kids. She seemed to have the perfect life."

One day Smith snapped some photographs of Mikey at play, submitting them to his editor, who published them. Karen was delighted, asking him if he would take a family portrait when her parents next visited.

"I took the picture outside on the lawn," he said. "The whole family was so loving, but I thought it was kind of odd that Dr. Sharpe wasn't there."

By January 1999, Dr. Sharpe was established in his new office and the new cosmetic side of the business was making so much money, he set up a new company called LaseHair. He based it at Great Ledge Lane with Karen as president. He hired his brother Bob to set up a sophisticated new computer network for the expanded operation. He personally designed the Web site, using a sexy picture of his daughter Shannon, in a slinky low-cut dress, to attract customers.

"Shannon Sharpe holds a Bachelor of Science degree and is a Certified Laser Technician," boasted his site. "In addition Shannon performs personalized and compassionate laser consultations and treatments."

"He picked the pictures out for the Web site," said Feeney, "and the wording was very seductive. Shannon didn't even realize it until her boyfriend pointed out that it was really inappropriate."

Most weekends Sharpe and Feeney would tour the various affiliates, and during their long hours together driving around Massachusetts they became friends. The doctor even gave her his Pathfinder SUV, when her own car broke down, although she would later complain that he used her like a taxi service, ferrying liposuction patients to and from his practice to the Cape Ann Marina, where he'd book them into a room to recuperate.

"He used to tell me things about his childhood and his father," she remembered. "My own dad had just died in July and he comforted me, telling me how hard it had been when his mom passed away from cancer some years earlier."

Sharpe seemed near tears, telling her how the retired

Benjamin Sharpe had nursed his dying wife for a year until her death in the mid-1980s. Several years later Benjamin had suffered a stroke, dying alone in a Shelton nursing home.

"Rich said he needed to prove himself to his father to feel accepted," said Feeney. "And he never got the chance to show him what he had done. He never once said his father had hit him as a child."

That winter, Richard Sharpe hired two young men as marketing executives for Clickmed. Based in a small office at his practice, they cold-called all over America, selling his patented HealthTrack software. The official 1999 company report shows the ClickMed corporation now had annual sales of 2 million dollars.

Streams of patients would pass through his frenetic office for cosmetic procedures and surgery. Between appointments Dr. Sharpe would check the progress of his shares on the computer, congratulating himself if they were doing well.

"You could see his mind going in five different directions," said Jacqui Feeney. "Somehow he managed to keep ten balls up in the air at once."

Dr. Sharpe was a passionate Beatles fan and always played their music on the office stereo while he performed liposuction.

"I used to kid him that Charlie Manson loved the Beatles too," said Feeney. "And he thought that was very funny."

Soon after founding LaseHair, Dr. Sharpe ventured into more dubious business territory, where he made even more money. He bought a Microdermabrasion machine for skin rejuvenation, in which minute crystals are sprayed with great force over the skin, and then vacuumed off, giving the skin a more youthful look. He carefully researched the expensive crystals sold by the manufacturers, discovering that they had the same chemical composition as aluminum oxide, used by body shops to sand-blast cars.

Dr. Sharpe saw dollar signs and bulk ordered huge quantities of sand-blast, selling it online to other professionals at a fraction of the regular price. He even had his staff repackage the crystals, using labels of his own design.

Fired with enthusiasm, he then discovered that cryogen, an expensive coolant used to operate lasers, had the very same ingredient used in automobile air conditioners. Although by law he was supposed to be licensed to sell cryogen, that didn't stop him from ordering huge tanks of the stuff, and selling it on the Internet at big discounts.

But he did have problems transferring the cryogen from the large containers in which it was sold to garages, into the smaller laser bottles for medical use. So he called in Jacqui Feeney's boyfriend Scott Kilman, a self-employed plumber and heating contractor, to help him solve the problem, after first attempting to heat up the freezing cryogen in his kitchen oven.

"He damn near blew the house up," remembered Kilman. "Then he figured it out using a cube heater."

Once he had perfected cryogen transferral, he ordered hundreds of the bottles for his own lasers. When they were empty, he had Kilman refill them, sticking on new labels.

As soon as he advertised cryogen on his Web site at a fraction of the regular price, he was swamped with orders.

"We couldn't keep up," said Feeney. "We were working out of his office, and I was shipping it all over America."

Then, believing that ClickMed—the company he sold the cryogen through—would be an attractive buy for the medical giant Candela Corporation, he floated it on the market.

"He tried to take a run at it, and quite frankly, he didn't get too far," said Candela president Jerry Puorro. "He contacted our sales guy to see if I would have lunch with him to see if I would buy ClickMed. I wouldn't buy ClickMed or his lunch."

Furious at being snubbed, Sharpe launched an attack on Candela, threatening to sue the company for anti-trust violations in respect to unfair sales methods.

In early 2000, Dr. Sharpe claimed he was now worth 5 million dollars. And although Karen still had no clue about the vast quantities of money his various companies were now generating, she was becoming increasingly alarmed about the legality of his business practices. As president of LaseHair, she realized *she* would be in trouble if they were ever audited.

"She was so worried," said Connie Behnke, to whom she confided her fears. "The whole LaseHair and liposuction was a cash business and there was no paper trail. She felt he was doing real illegal things with taxes and could get them both into serious trouble, as he was not declaring most of what he was making."

Although Dr. Sharpe had more money than he could spend, his staff thought him unusually tight with a buck. He'd nickel-and-dime everyone, paying minimum wages and working his technicians and nurses into the ground. But he would try to buy friendship. Soon after Jacqui Feeney began working for him, he insisted on buying her a membership at an expensive gym in Danvers, so he would have someone to work out with.

"At first I wasn't sure about working out with him,

as he was my boss," she said. "But after we became friends, we went all the time with Shannon and another girl he knew."

One day Feeney noticed Dr. Sharpe wore lacy Victoria's Secret panties under his form-fitting spandex tights, which he then carefully tucked his t-shirt into.

"We told him that he had a body any woman would kill for," she said. "Not meaning that a woman would want his body, but they'd wish they had his legs or his thighs."

Apparently delighted to hear this, Dr. Sharpe confided how he and Karen had gone to a Halloween party as sisters and had "mad" sex afterwards. But when he offered to show her pictures of himself in full drag, she refused, afraid he would ask her to participate in some weird sex game.

"I didn't like it," she said. "I think he was trying to bounce this off me and see my reaction. If I had responded more positively, he might have opened up more, but because I was so repulsed he changed the subject."

In January 2000, Jacqui and Karen accompanied him to a two-day conference for trans-gendered individuals at the Woburn Park Plaza, where they manned the LaseHair booth. Although Dr. Sharpe was scheduled to perform a Botox procedure, he disappeared on the second day, reappearing in the evening wearing full makeup and eyeliner.

"He said someone had talked him into putting on this dress," remembered Jacqui. "He was so delighted he fitted into a size three, and wanted to show me the pictures. That was the last thing I wanted to see. I think he was trying to introduce me to the idea a little bit at a time, to see if I would accept it."

When Jacqui told Scott Kilman about her boss's obsession with women's clothes, he checked out Dr. Sharpe's personal computer the next time he was alone in the office.

"It was the squeakiest-clean computer I had seen in my life," said Kilman. "Not one pornography site anywhere, and believe me, I can find them."

Chapter Ten

A BRIGHT LIGHT
AT THE END OF THE TUNNEL

In November 1999, a LaseHair affiliate named Leigh Adams told Dr. Sharpe about a spacious colonial-style house in Wenham that was on the market. Its owner had run out of cash to finish it off and was desperate to sell, due to a divorce. Sharpe asked Karen to go and check it out and she took Connie Behnke. Lying seven miles west of Gloucester, three exits away on Route 128, a long driveway led up to the stately two-story structure, which stood on its own grounds near a pond.

Richard and Karen would both later deny ever wanting to buy 19 Hull Street, claiming they were each persuaded by the other. Nevertheless, on December 19, Dr. Sharpe bought it for $535,000, taking out a $15,000 construction loan a month later, and getting a second mortgage on Great Ledge Lane.

Later, Dr. Sharpe would label the house "decadent," claiming Karen had browbeaten him into buying it.

"I wanted to semi-retire and work just two days a week instead of seven," he would say. "I wanted to spend more time with my children."

Whatever the truth, Karen threw herself into finishing

off the house, hiring a local contractor named Marc Beauregard, enthusiastically selecting the fittings and color schemes. The Sharpes planned to move in together in May when work was completed.

"She loved all this," said Behnke. "But I think it was the kind of a job where she could get away from him and feel good about herself."

Karen also rallied around her friend Cynthia Goodhew, whose nineteen-year-old son was diagnosed with cancer. As a trained nurse, she went along to all his doctor appointments, single-handedly organizing a fund-raiser at a local Elks Lodge to help pay his medical bills.

That Christmas, Karen's family came to Great Ledge Lane for the final holiday get-together before they moved into their new Wenham house. It was the first time they had visited over Christmas for years, and as usual Richard Sharpe was his bad-tempered self, wanting to be the center of attention.

"I remember Michael had gotten a Howard airplane," said his grandfather, John Hatfield. "And Rich just grabbed it, took it outside to fly and ended up breaking it."

Little Mikey was in tears, so his Uncle John went outside and gathered up the pieces of the broken model plane, managing to repair it. Once again his father snatched the plane away from him and threw it into the air, breaking it beyond repair.

"He was a terrible father," said Hatfield Sr. "He did not treat the children well, and they did not like him. That was perfectly obvious from when we'd be around there."

In February 2000, Dr. Sharpe was threatened with a lawsuit from a rival company over his LaseHair Web site. So on February 10, on the advice of an estate planning lawyer, he transferred $2.9 million from his Fidelity

Brokerage account over to Karen's name, as well as the new Wenham house, as a hedge against possible legal action.

Overnight Karen became a wealthy woman in her own right, for the first time realizing the full extent of their worth. Suddenly she felt empowered, and the whole dynamic of their tumultuous relationship began to shift.

"It's almost like a light bulb went off," remembered Connie Behnke. " 'I've got the Wenham house. I've got the money in my name.' She was really feeling good about herself."

At this time Karen began seeing a local psychiatrist named Dr. Mitchell Cohen, who was horrified as she recounted her history of marital abuse. He suggested she join a local abused women's group, but she refused.

She also fell in love with her builder, Marc Beauregard, basking in the attention she so craved.

"He showed interest in her," said Behnke. "She found someone that was, in her mind, sunny, articulate and handsome. That he thought she was attractive meant a lot to her, and she was really excited about it."

Karen suddenly seemed to have taken out a new lease on life, and when Karen Beswick asked her why, she told her about Beauregard.

"You know how that new love is," said the headmistress. "You could see it all over her, and it gave her the confidence she needed."

During the last week of February, two separate incidents happened that finally drove Karen out of her miserable marriage. Lately Richard Sharpe had taken to staying out all night, returning home in the early morning, still wearing full make-up. Things came to a head when seven-year-old Michael was getting ready to go to school and his father came through the front door, wearing smudgy red lipstick and mascara.

"Get upstairs!" yelled Karen, furiously. "Don't you ever let your son see you that way."

Soon afterwards, she told Connie she could no longer tolerate his cross-dressing and had to protect Mikey, who was at an impressionable age.

Then, conspiratorially, she took Connie to their bedroom and showed her a box, containing $700 worth of French silk pantyhose her husband had recently bought himself.

"She said it had become so weird and she didn't know where he was going all night."

Karen also confided that he was taking her birth control pills and had breasts, saying she had no idea if he was planning to have a sex-change operation.

The following Sunday, Shannon, who was living in the guest suite at Great Ledge Lane, discovered that her father had mysteriously purchased duct tape and hoses, which he'd left in the kitchen. Later in an affidavit, she wrote she was so alarmed, she immediately called her mother and they assumed the worst: that Richard Sharpe was finally planning to carry out his threat to kill his family.

Later that night Jacqui Feeney arrived at Great Ledge Lane to pick up some equipment, and Karen sat her down, telling her she wanted a divorce.

"She said, 'I've made up my mind, I'm leaving him,' " remembered Feeney. "She told me that I could go upstairs and talk to him, and that he was in the fetal position. I thought she was being sarcastic."

Feeney then went upstairs to discover her boss distraught, curled up on the bed just as Karen had described. He told her he was waiting for Karen to come back so they could talk.

"I was really shocked," she said. "And then when I left, Karen said to me, 'What he needs is a girlfriend or a boyfriend.' "

On Monday, February 28, 2000, Karen Sharpe secretly made arrangements to walk out of her tortured marriage with Mikey and Ali. She found a divorce lawyer and made reservations for the three of them that evening at the Liberty Motel in North Beverly, fifteen miles west of Gloucester.

That afternoon Connie Behnke was flying into Boston from Wisconsin, and Karen picked her up at the airport. On the way home Karen asked if Connie could babysit Mikey and Ali for a couple of hours, as she was going home to pack her bags and leave.

"I was flabbergasted," remembered Behnke. "But I was thrilled she was leaving."

When Connie asked where she would be taking Mikey and Ali, Karen refused to tell her, so she wouldn't have to lie if Dr. Sharpe called her.

"Connie, you don't know what he's capable of," Karen told her. "He'll take us all down. That's the kind of person he is."

At about 5:00 p.m. Richard Sharpe returned to Great Ledge Lane. He had spent the day seeing patients at his practice and had skipped the gym, feeling as if he was coming down with a cold. Mikey and Ali were playing in the upstairs sunroom, so he went downstairs to the kitchen, where Karen made him a cup of tea.

For the next hour Karen bravely kept a poker face as she made small talk, constantly on her guard not to let something slip. Finally she suggested he go upstairs and rest, promising to bring him up a snack and a cup of tea later. As Sharpe dozed off in front of the television, watching CNN, Karen scooped up Mikey and Ali and made her escape in her car.

At about 9:30 p.m. he awoke and went downstairs, finding the house deserted. Thinking Karen had taken the two children to the store, he made himself a cup of tea and went back upstairs. But when they hadn't returned an hour later he tried Karen's two cell phones and failed to get an answer.

"I started freaking out," he would later testify. "I was bouncing off the walls."

He then called his attorney Karen Sweeney Shea, who told him Karen might have gotten mad and taken off. So he got on the Internet, tracking down the numbers for all the hotels within a twenty-mile radius of Gloucester. He was on the phone until three in the morning without success, before calling Jacqui Feeney in tears.

"He was just losing it," she remembered. "He kept telling me she had left with the kids and he just didn't know where she was."

By first thing Tuesday morning, Richard was composed enough to try to buy Shannon's support against her mother. He had his attorney immediately draw up a contract "selling" her the valuable Cambridge condominium, worth an estimated $750,000, for a token payment of just one dollar. It also brought in $1,500 a month in rent, making the twenty-six-year-old wealthy.

"As soon as Karen left, the first thing he did was to start doing these incredible power plays with her," said Connie Behnke. "I'm sure that condo in Cambridge was partly a way of solidifying his support with Shannon. It was like getting a million dollars."

And when Shannon accepted the condo and remained working and living with her father, Karen was crushed. Although Shannon would later maintain that she had only stayed to "keep a watchful eye on Richard" and warn her mother "if I suspected any wrong-doing," Karen told friends it was "a bitter blow."

"She would have done anything for Shannon," said Behnke. "She just loved her kids so much. But that was something that was very hard for her."

Shannon's Aunt Kathleen says she only pretended to side with her father, so she could keep an eagle eye on him and not lose his trust, and gather information that her mother could use.

"And I think Shannon still feels guilty about the fact that she stayed there, but she was doing the right thing," said her aunt.

On Tuesday morning, Karen called Kathleen at work with the news that she had finally walked out on the marriage, saying she was starting a new life with Mikey and Ali.

"Well, I've finally done it," she told her sister triumphantly. "I've left him, and that's that."

Kathleen told her she was delighted that she had finally made the break, asking where she was hiding out with the children and if she needed anything. Karen said she was in a hotel until the new house in Wenham was finished and they could move in. But she refused to reveal her whereabouts, so that Sharpe couldn't intimidate her.

"I told her that it wasn't going to be easy," said Kathleen. "She said she knew, but she had a good lawyer."

Immediately after putting down the phone Kathleen called her eldest daughter at their home in Beacon Falls, Connecticut, telling her to call 911 if her Uncle Richie turned up at the house, and on no account to talk to him.

"There were a couple of occasions when Karen had left him for a day or two," she said, "and he's turned up on our doorstep, saying he missed her and needed her, making himself seem like a poor lost soul."

Her brother Jamie tried to bolster her spirits, saying that she would soon have a new life.

"She saw a very bright light at the end of the tunnel," he remembered. "But at the same time I sensed fear in the fact that she was going to move into that house two exits away from him, and seeing how controlling he always was."

That afternoon, Karen called Sharpe from the Beverly motel where she was staying with Mikey and Ali, demanding a divorce. She refused to reveal where they were, saying he could see his children when she was ready. Then she put down the phone, promising to call again soon.

Desperate to get Karen and his children back under his control, Dr. Sharpe hired a private investigator to track her down and follow her. He also started lurking outside the Shannah Montessori School, guessing correctly that Karen was still taking Mikey and Ali to and from there each day.

Mikey and Ali loved living in the motel away from their father. And their headmistress, Karen Beswick, saw a drastic change in their behavior once they were free of him.

"Mikey was so happy living in a motel," said Beswick. "Karen said he had told her how happy he was not to be living with dad anymore."

Karen also seemed transformed, decorating the Wenham home and making plans for the future.

"It was probably the most difficult time, and yet the most exciting time for her," Beswick remembered. "I think she felt like a new woman because she was free for the first time in I don't know how many years."

But if Karen was ecstatically happy after she left, Richard Sharpe was plumbing the depths of despair, gobbling Xanax and other prescription drugs and drinking heavily. One night, soon after she left, he took Shannon, Jacqui Feeney and Scott Kilman out for dinner at Tom Sheas Seafood Restaurant in Essex. Throughout the meal he passed around the table a Tic Tac packet containing a new supply of Xanax he had ordered.

"It was like a funeral," remembered Feeney. "We were all upset. We thought Karen was cracking up, because nobody could understand it. He was trying to sedate everybody and I said jokingly, 'You'd better watch it with the Tic Tacs.' "

The following day, Karen met with her estranged husband on neutral territory in his lawyer's office, bringing along Mikey and Ali. Pale and drawn, Sharpe tearfully pleaded with Karen to try to work things out, but she remained adamant that she wanted a divorce.

After the meeting, a furious Dr. Sharpe moved fast to try to cut off Karen's funds. Realizing that once she filed for divorce, all their assets would be legally frozen, he forged her signature on a withdrawal slip to transfer $2.1 million out of her Fidelity account into his son Michael's trust. But he was thwarted when the brokerage house called Karen to confirm the transaction, and she had it stopped.

He also instructed his lawyer to cut her out of his will without a cent.

"He forged her name to transfer the money into irrevocable trust," said Connie Behnke, who was in daily telephone contact with Karen while she was at the motel. "She knew nothing about that, and she was absolutely livid when she found out."

That weekend Karen and her divorce lawyer met Sharpe at Great Ledge Lane to hammer out an agreement for him to have access to Mikey and Ali.

"I wanted to put the divorce and separation on hold for two months, so we could sort things out and maybe reconcile," he said. "Karen said absolutely not. She didn't want to put anything on hold."

Sharpe sat there helplessly as an empowered Karen took control of the situation. She told him that he could never again set foot in the Wenham house and only have limited visitation rights to his two young children.

"I didn't know if she was on drugs or something," he would later say. "We had a very emotional, long drawn-out argument, where I accused her of using me as a meal ticket."

While Karen was talking to her attorney at Great Ledge Lane, Dr. Sharpe rifled through her pocketbook, finding keys and a receipt for the Liberty Motel. He also searched the glove compartment of her Ford Expedition, finding some financial papers, which he placed in his Mustang. He also took her motel key and had it copied, later replacing it in her pocketbook, without her knowing.

On Friday, March 3, Dr. Sharpe was having coffee at a Dunkin' Donuts when he overheard two workmen discussing how their boss was "porking a rich bitch in Wenham," and realized they were referring to Karen and Marc Beauregard.

"Then I put two and two together," he would later testify. "I hoped it wasn't true. I was a wreck. Just a wreck."

A few days later a teller at Fleet Bank told him that Marc Beauregard was regularly cashing multiple checks signed by Richard's estranged wife.

Infuriated by what he had heard, he fired Karen as president of LaseHair, ordering her to turn over all the company's records. He replaced her with an affiliate, Betsy Brown (not her real name), with a salary of

$100,000 a year. Later, when Karen refused to hand over the records, he would accuse her of embezzling money from the company, and giving Beauregard money for building work that was never done.

Chapter Eleven

THE BELLY OF THE BEAST

On Sunday, March 5, at 10:00 p.m., Dr. Richard Sharpe was carrying his portable laser diode up to his office at Great Ledge Lane to repair it, when he lost his balance and fell down a flight of stairs. He blacked out, later regaining consciousness to find the heavy laser machinery lying on top of him.

"I was in a lot of pain and couldn't get up," he remembered. "Eventually I crawled into the living room and buzzed Shannon for help."

Shannon called an ambulance to take him to Beverly Hospital, where he was admitted. He was diagnosed with a concussion, and a broken pelvis and tailbone, as well as aggravating an old back injury.

"Rich called me in the middle of the night to say that he had fallen down the stairs," said Jacqui Feeney. "He was always clumsy, but he was also taking pills because he was bumming out."

During his week in the hospital he was given the strong painkiller Demerol, but he remained coherent enough to hatch an elaborate plan to break into Karen's motel room, enlisting the help of Jacqui's boyfriend,

Scott Kilman. He now planned to take the initiative and serve Karen with divorce papers first, and was looking for any evidence that might help.

"He telephoned and asked me if I wanted to make five hundred dollars," remembered Kilman. "He told me to meet him at North Beverly train station and not to tell Jacqui."

As soon as he got off the phone Kilman told his girlfriend, and they agreed that he should meet Dr. Sharpe and see what he wanted.

The following morning, Wednesday, March 8, Richard signed himself out of the hospital and hobbled out on crutches, hiring a blue Pontiac rent-a-wreck. He drove straight to the North Beverly station, within view of the Liberty Motel, where Karen and the children were hiding, rendezvousing with Kilman in the parking lot.

"He said, 'I want you to break into a hotel room,' and showed me the key, telling me how he got it," said Kilman. "He said Karen had up to $100,000 of his cash and other financial documents that she had stolen. I was astonished that he would ask me, and I left. Again he told me not to tell Jacqueline anything about it."

After Kilman left, Sharpe reclined his car seat so he couldn't be seen and waited for Karen and the children to leave the motel. When he saw them go, and the coast was clear, he drove over to the motel, parked outside their room and went inside.

Later he would testify that he only found out which room Karen was in when he saw her leave. Somewhat incredibly, he would claim her door had been left open, allowing him to gain access. He never mentioned copying her key.

"[I was inside] four or five minutes," he said. "I took a day timer with some phone numbers."

Careful not to be seen, he then got back in his rented

car and drove back to Beverly Hospital, where he fainted in the lobby and was immediately readmitted.

On Thursday, March 9, Richard's attorney surprised Karen Sharpe with divorce papers at the Liberty Motel. He also filed for custody of Mikey and Ali.

Karen was livid and began calling her attorney in a panic, but she became frustrated at being constantly fobbed off with office clerks.

"She wanted someone that would look after her interests," said Connie. "Then I suggested Jacob Atwood."

Affectionately known in Boston legal circles as "Jake the Snake," Atwood was reputed to be *the* toughest divorce lawyer in the state, ruthlessly winning case after case. When Karen drove to Boston and met with him for the first time at his office at Dexter House on Commonwealth Avenue, she knew she had found the right man to champion her in her oncoming battle, even if she might sometimes question the tactics he employed.

An unabashed Anglophile, Jacob Atwood ruled his legal domain from a large, elaborate wooden throne. Standing guard outside his baronial-style second-floor office sat a full suit of medieval knight's armor. The bulky, ruddy-faced lawyer's lofty taste of office décor reflected his hobby of building and restoring eighteenth-century homes to their former glory.

With forty-five years' experience at the Boston bar, the sixty-nine-year-old lawyer co-founded Atwood & Cherny, one of the nation's leading family law practices.

"Even Karen found him too much," said Behnke. "But she said he's the best one and great at what he does."

At one of their first meetings, Karen swore out a fifteen-page client narrative, detailing the years of savage abuse and battering she had endured. But she insisted that it be kept secret, still remaining loyal to Richard under the most difficult of circumstances.

Atwood immediately sprang into action, firing off a counterclaim on Karen's behalf, suing Dr. Sharpe for divorce and custody and support of Mikey and Ali. It accused him of being "guilty of cruel and abusive treatment" on numerous occasions during their marriage, culminating on March 2, when she fled the marital home. Atwood's claim also called for at least $20,000 to cover his services, saying that Karen was unemployed and almost penniless.

"The husband has virtually unlimited funds," read the counterclaim, "and it is only fair and equitable that the wife, her counsel, and her experts have the same opportunity to litigate."

It would be the first volley in the ensuing divorce battle which would quickly escalate to almost biblical proportions.

After he was finally discharged from the hospital in mid-March, Dr. Sharpe stopped seeing patients, saying he could no longer cope with the stress. When he stopped going to Harvard Medical School he was told his teaching services were no longer needed.

Largely immobile with chronic back pain, he spent his days camped out on a couch in the living room. Betsy Brown was now running LaseHair from the basement, and every so often she would come up and ask his advice, to make him feel involved. When he told LaseHair employees he could no longer pay their wages, his bookkeeper Suzanne Crossen, receptionist Rose Horne and nurse Ellen Flaherty resigned en masse.

"I was out of it and not very responsive," he would later explain. "The whole period was a blur."

But Jacqui Feeney felt sorry for her boss, visiting his

house every day to take care of him. She drove him back to Beverly Hospital for his MRI, where doctors discovered he was suffering from double pneumonia and readmitted him for several days' more treatment.

But finally even Jacqui became fed up with catering to Sharpe's ever-increasing demands, and handed in her notice. Before she left, he asked her to find the file of a long-time patient named Paula Hiltz. Somehow he had heard that the young mother had recently been thrown out by her boyfriend, and urgently needed a place to stay. He saw her as the perfect replacement for Feeney.

"He was trying to talk her into coming and working for him," said Feeney. "And then she basically moved in."

A plain girl with mousy colored hair, Hiltz had been engaged to a local welder named Alden Tarr Jr. for the previous seven years, and they had a five-year-old son named Audie. But the relationship had broken up in August 1999 and she was now desperate to move out of his home at 108 Washington Street, Gloucester.

Paula readily took the job as Dr. Sharpe's receptionist and moved into Great Ledge Lane at the beginning of April, sleeping on a couch and occasionally sharing his bed.

"I answered the phones," she explained. "I just booked appointments and did some balancing of the day sheets."

Shannon was off on a trip to Asia, seeking new business opportunities for LaseHair, and Paula soon filled a void in Dr. Sharpe's life. She began looking after him, later becoming his girlfriend.

"Quite often I'd work late in the evening," she explained, "and we'd go out and grab a bite to eat. Then I would come back and work again."

During their meals after work, Paula spoke about her

ex-fiancé Alden Tarr, complaining that he had been far more interested in his gun collection than he had ever been in her. On hearing this, Dr. Sharpe asked her about his collection, discovering that Tarr had several shotguns and rifles in his living room. He also noted that Paula had the keys to his house and safe, where he kept his ammunition.

As Dr. Richard Sharpe was getting back on his feet, he fired LaseHair's new president Betsy Brown, after hearing that she was attempting to set up her own rival hair removal business to compete with his. To replace her he hired an experienced Florida-based business consultant named Richard Fonte, putting him in charge of running the company and later appointing him president.

"I just turned everything over to Rich Fonte," said Sharpe. "He was pretty thorough, though."

Fonte, a former vice president with Timex International, who had been suggested for the job by Ben Sharpe, made a detailed analysis of the company books. He warned Sharpe that LaseHair was almost broke and unless there was an immediate cash injection, it would go under.

During their business meetings, Dr. Sharpe would often get emotional, recounting how Karen had left with the kids, and how upset he was.

"He was upset about the divorce," said Fonte. "He was upset about his children being taken away from him."

Fonte would later testify Dr. Sharpe also told him how Karen was living with her builder boyfriend Marc Beauregard, and giving him money for nonexistent work.

On March 27 the Salem Probate and Family Court ruled that the couple should temporarily share custody of Mikey and Ali, although they would continue living with their mother. Richard Sharpe would be allowed visitations for two hours every Monday and Wednesday afternoon, and mornings every other weekend. He was also given permission to telephone them on evenings when he could not see them.

When Mikey and Ali heard that they would still have to see their father, they burst into tears. And it would be a constant battle for Karen to make them go to the court-ordered play dates at Great Ledge Lane.

Chapter Twelve

EVIL GENIUS

At the beginning of April, Karen Sharpe and her children moved into the new house at 19 Hull Street. Although the extensive renovations were still not completely finished, enough rooms were habitable to live in comfortably. Soon after arriving, she introduced herself to her new neighbors, David and Lane Sabatini, who had a nine-year-old son and a seven-year-old daughter. The two families immediately hit it off, becoming firm friends and regularly visiting each other's homes. They soon established a routine where Karen would call the Sabatini home every morning at 8:00 a.m., saying: "Get the kids over here, I'm making pancakes."

Then, as the two mothers chatted in the kitchen, Mikey and Ali would play by the pond with the Sabatini kids.

"Her whole life was centered around those children and her children's friends," said Lane.

Soon after Karen and the children moved into the Wenham house, she invited her family over to visit. There was an underlying feeling of relief that Richard wasn't there anymore to make his presence felt, although

Karen always looked for signs that he might be secretly watching.

The family gatherings were some of the rare happy times during this difficult period for Mikey and Ali. It was a new generation of Camp Hatfield, as the family enjoyed barbecues, played Trivial Pursuit and hiked in the forests around Wenham.

The week before Easter, Karen took her kids to her sister Kathleen's Connecticut house for a family gathering. At first she had tried to cancel, telling Kathleen that she feared Rich would arrive and pull one of his stunts.

"And I was very emphatic with her," said Kathleen. "I said, 'You know what? If he's going to pull something, I'd rather it be here than up in Massachusetts.' "

After they arrived it took Karen a few hours to relax, as she constantly peered through the window, expecting to see Richard's car pulling up to the house. But when she finally calmed down they had a great time, with Karen organizing an Easter egg hunt for the kids.

"He never showed," said Kathleen. "But although we never saw him, that still doesn't mean he wasn't there. He was capable of anything."

Now, carving out a new life for herself and her children, Karen seemed happier and more positive than she had in many years. But inwardly she was filled with self-doubt. Her relationship with Beauregard was not going well, and she began to realize that he wasn't quite the knight in shining armor she had thought.

"He'd make a date and wouldn't call or show up," said Connie Behnke, who'd met the builder during an Italian restaurant dinner Karen had organized to introduce him to her friends. "She'd get a babysitter and get all dressed up, and he'd never even pick up a phone to say he couldn't make it. It happened over and over again."

On April 21, the Friday before Easter, Dr. Sharpe was having a barbecue with Paula Hiltz and one of his LaseHair affiliates, when Karen telephoned, asking to come over to talk.

"Karen had been fairly distant, not very cooperative on any level," he would later testify. "Her tone of voice was different."

According to Sharpe, she came over and they had an emotional reconciliation, with Karen agreeing to give him another chance.

"Well, we talked," he said. "We were sitting close together and then we started hugging each other and kissing. We couldn't take our hands off each other and ended up making love that night. It was almost like we were on a honeymoon."

The following day, Dr. Sharpe moved into 19 Hull Street, spending the next four days on his best behavior with Karen, Mikey and Ali. He asked Karen about Marc Beauregard and she told him how the builder had given her the attention she needed, and Richard had failed to give her, during their marriage.

He deftly steered the conversation to money, asking what she had done with the 2.9 million dollars that she still had in the Fidelity account. She said it was in good hands, and Jacob Atwood had suggested a financial advisor who was helping her re-invest the money.

Sharpe said he could do better, pressuring Karen to transfer 2 million dollars into his Merrill Lynch account. When she finally agreed to his demands, he moved fast, arranging for a financial advisor to come around immediately with the necessary paperwork, which she duly signed.

"I mean, money wasn't really a major priority," he

would later claim. "I was happy to get my family back. Happy to have my wife back." But Karen would claim the reconciliation was "merely a guise to procure access" to the money.

By Wednesday, Karen realized that she had made a huge mistake in agreeing to go back to Richard. She ordered him out, vowing to divorce him. For the next six hours he begged and pleaded for her to stay, before finally giving up and storming out of the house.

"Karen called me up and said, 'What was I thinking?' " said Connie Behnke. "She felt really dreadful about that and said it was not going to happen again."

Kathleen Lembo was also horrified when Shannon told her about the reconciliation. And when she asked, Karen told her how he had turned up at Hull Street and she'd let him sleep there, telling him to leave the next morning.

"Again, he's preying on her, thinking it would be the same kiss-and-make-up thing that used to happen in the past," said Kathleen. "But she was beyond that."

Karen told her sister she had only come to her senses after little Mikey broke down in tears, saying that he couldn't stand them yelling all the time.

After Sharpe left, Karen called Jacob Atwood, who cancelled the $2 million transfer on her behalf, claiming in a letter to Merrill Lynch that it had been signed under "considerable emotional duress and undue influence."

"Now that Ms. Sharpe has had the benefit of legal guidance and advice," wrote Atwood, "it is her will to cancel any paperwork which she was coerced to sign. You are hereby instructed to forthwith desist and refrain from attempting to transfer her funds to any other account of any nature whatsoever."

For the first time ever in their twenty-seven-year marriage, Richard Sharpe had failed to entice Karen back into his clutches, and he began to realize that he could no longer control her. Now he resolved to enlist Mikey and Ali in his battle to dominate Karen, using his own children as innocent pawns in an all-out war to destroy her.

"Rich just could not grasp it," said Connie Behnke. "It was all about him having control of Karen. Now there was some realization that he had run out of ways to manipulate her. That *she* had the power this time, the money and the attorney."

In May, Dr. Sharpe escalated his campaign to wear Karen down. He started following her, spending hours staking out Hull Street, checking for signs of Marc Beauregard. He also called her day and night, making his presence felt. Now if Lane Sabatini wanted a chat with her neighbor, she had to walk over to the house, as Karen's phone was always off the hook.

"Eventually, I turned the ringer off on both telephones to alleviate this harassment," Karen wrote. "Richard has been shadowing many of my activities and has told me that he hired someone to follow me. On one occasion in recent weeks, my husband pursued me in his automobile while I was driving with the children. Fearful of the circumstances, I contacted my attorneys and requested that they contact opposing counsel to diffuse the situation."

Late one night, Dr. Sharpe sneaked up the long Hull Street driveway to where Karen's Ford Expedition was parked, removing the plates and then canceling her car insurance. She was now driving illegally and faced arrest. When she drove the children to her parents' house in Shelton the next weekend without plates or insurance, she was livid when she discovered what he had done.

"She was really, really upset," said Karen Beswick,

to whom she had tearfully confided the incident. "I'd never seen her that bad."

And Karen's psychiatrist, Dr. Mitchell Cohen, was becoming increasingly concerned about her, and her growing fears that her husband would murder her. He urged her to get a restraining order against Sharpe for her own protection, saying her current situation was "highly volatile and dangerous."

Karen agreed, reluctantly giving Atwood permission to file her affidavit with probate court, containing the horrific secrets of her marriage that she had never told anyone.

"[She] knew her kids were frightened by his behavior," wrote Dr. Cohen the first week of May. "She can't stand it [but is] not suicidal."

The psychiatrist also suggested she visit the Gloucester chapter of Help for Abused Women and their Children (HAWC), but she refused.

During one emotional session in mid-May, she told Dr. Mitchell about how her husband had once stabbed her with a fork, and how he had beaten her up, after his brother had thrown him out of his New Year's Eve party.

"Two stories of horror from past of horrendous abuse and his threatening to kill her," wrote Dr. Cohen in his notes. "Teary, but aware that telling the story good for her and she no longer has an alternative."

Karen also told him of her husband's "coldness" and her confusion at the mixed messages he was sending.

"He has a girlfriend but says he wants her back," wrote Dr. Cohen. "Terrible that people would tend to not help even when she was beaten and broken. Part of why she kept secret so long."

On May 17, the Essex Division of the Probate and Family Court granted Karen a restraining order against Richard Sharpe. Under threat of imprisonment he was ordered not to contact or abuse her, and forbidden from entering 19 Hull Street. From now on he would have to pick up and drop off Mikey and Ali from the curbside outside the home.

Karen was terrified he would turn up at the Shannah Montessori school and kidnap her children. She told Karen Beswick of her fears, and together they drafted a letter so the headmistress would not be legally bound to release Mikey and Ali to their father.

A few nights later, Dr. Sharpe was out drinking with Paula Hiltz when he had her drive by Hull Street, so he could see if Marc Beauregard was there.

"I saw his truck in the driveway," he would later testify. "I asked Paula to stop and I said I was just going to visit for a few minutes."

Sensing trouble, Paula tried to talk him out of it, but he refused. Sharpe would later claim his original plan had been to "barge in" and confront the couple, but he knew it would breach the restraining order, meaning automatic arrest.

"I looked in various windows and the two of them were on the couch, and Mikey and Ali were running around," he remembered. "I became very angry."

He picked up a rock, smashing the headlights on Beauregard's truck. Then he hurried back to his car, telling Paula to drive off as fast as she could. When she mentioned hearing a noise and asked if he had knocked on Karen's front door, he evaded her questions, remaining silent for the short drive back to Gloucester.

Although the incident was never reported to the police, it traumatized Karen. She now started telling close friends she feared for her life, and that Richard was having her followed constantly.

Dr. Cohen's entry for his May 23 session with Karen reveals the toll Sharpe's terror campaign was taking.

It read: "Frightened. Afraid Rich will kill her, obsessed with her being followed. A feeling that he is an evil genius and she will never be free of him. Her best friends don't even know nearly how bad it is. She is busy protecting everyone on the planet except herself. Mentioned HAWC again."

Now, prosecutors believe, Dr. Sharpe made up his mind that if he couldn't have Karen, no one else would. He began looking for a shotgun, somehow obtaining a .22-caliber rifle from an unknown source.

As the divorce dragged on through June, becoming uglier at every turn, Jacob Atwood turned the pressure up on Dr. Sharpe, trying to make him reveal his true worth, for an eventual settlement for Karen. When Sharpe repeatedly defied probate court orders to hand over his accounts, Atwood called for the court to appoint a discovery master to examine and value Richard's medical practice and all his other businesses.

"[Dr. Sharpe] has even suggested that he will intentionally prolong and stonewall the litigation process," wrote Atwood in his motion, claiming that Sharpe was still netting more than $100,000 a month from LaseHair and Clickmed.

The attorney also accused Sharpe of using his accident the previous month as an excuse to cancel several planned oral depositions, where he would have been questioned under oath by Atwood himself.

"In addition to frequently traveling to [Karen's] property, unannounced and uninvited," stated the motion, "[Dr. Sharpe] has traveled to the beach, frequented shopping malls and taken a recreational airplane ride at Beverly Airport."

Twice a week and on alternate weekends, Dr. Sharpe would collect Mikey and Ali from Wenham and take them back to his Gloucester home and spend time with them. While he had them there he would try to turn them against their mother.

"They didn't want to go on a visitation," said Connie Behnke. "And it was really hard for Karen to get them to go."

So to make things more comfortable for the children, it was agreed that Connie's kids, Natalie, Ellie and Emma, would also go along for the play dates, to keep Mikey and Ali company. While she was there, dropping off her kids and then collecting them, Dr. Sharpe would seek advice on a reconciliation, and then go off on a tirade, obsessed with the idea that Karen had taken his fortune.

"He talked about how angry he was that she, and these are his words, 'Stole my money,'" remembered Behnke. On one occasion she actually overheard Sharpe telling his seven-year-old son Mikey, "Your mother stole my money."

"Rich just didn't interact with them at all the way a normal father does," observed Behnke. "I really think he loved the little kids, [yet] this was a person who just never understood how to have a relationship that required his giving. He just didn't know how to give affection."

Although he would take them to Disney World and buy them pet dogs, cats and reptiles from a local store called Curious Creatures, Dr. Sharpe always appeared stiff and uncomfortable around his children.

"He'd never sit down and read a book and snuggle with them," she said. "Or lie on the floor and play a board game. He just didn't know how to do that stuff."

Then he would follow her to her car with a pathetic look on his face, whining: "Why is Karen doing this to me? I don't understand."

"It was always the same," she said. "Blaming Jacob Atwood for them being apart, and accusing her of taking all his money. It wasn't like he realized how much she meant to him and wanted to make it work, but more about how unfair it was that she had his hard-earned money."

On June 5, Dr. Sharpe's attorney, Karen Sweeney Shea, hit Karen with a barrage of motions to increase his access to the children and freeze all further building on Hull Street.

"He would never do anything to place the children at risk of harm," stated the motion. "He has always been a loving and attentive father."

The motion also maintained that Sharpe had now reduced his medications "except while experiencing exceptional pain," and had attended most of Mikey's sporting events before the restraining order prevented him from doing so. It demanded the probate and family court force Karen to pay him $20,000 to cover his legal expenses, claiming she had so mismanaged the almost 3 million dollars he had put in her name three months earlier, that it had dwindled down to $1.7 million.

"Karen's lack of financial knowledge and inability to properly manage the family finances has reduced our joint non-retirement assets," he stated in an attached affidavit.

Sharpe also used the court paper for an unsubstantiated attack on Karen's boyfriend Marc Beauregard, accusing him of not being a licensed construction supervisor or even being registered as a home improvement contractor. So far, it claimed, Beauregard had been paid more than $112,000 for work on the house, of which $50,500 was paid for by Karen's checks.

He also accused Karen of interfering in the running

of LaseHair, causing him to lose three important affiliates. "The business has suffered," it stated. "Since his accident [Dr. Sharpe] has been for the most part unable to continue practicing in his chosen field of Dermatology. He has, however, continued to attempt to run the business that he started as part of his practice two years ago."

Then, paraphrasing Jacob Atwood's own words when he had earlier demanded Sharpe pay $20,000 to cover attorney fees, the motion continued: "The Wife has virtually unlimited funds and it is only fair and equitable that the Husband, his counsel, and his experts have the same opportunity."

Besides his legal campaign to intimidate Karen, he was now having her followed, looking for further evidence to use against her in court.

"I believe I am being followed at my husband's directive," said Karen in an affidavit. "As recently as June 7th, when I traveled to retrieve our children from his residence, a Caucasian man in a black sedan, approximately six-feet-tall, two-hundred-pounds and approximately fifty-years-old, appeared to be watching me."

On June 12, Karen Sharpe renewed the restraining order and officially filed her damning twenty-three-point affidavit into probate court, laying bare the torturous secrets of her marriage. But even now, realizing the potential harm her accusations could do to her husband's medical career, Karen made Atwood lodge a separate motion, asking the court to impound the case file, so it never became public.

"Due to the nature of the Plaintiff's employment, he is fairly well-known within the community," it stated. "If particular aspects of this matter are made public, the consequences may be extremely detrimental."

Her new affidavit contained a supplemental paragraph, revealing for the first time Dr. Richard Sharpe's cross-dressing.

"My husband also exhibits transvestite tendencies," she wrote. "He is a cross-dresser and often wears female clothing. He has permanently removed all of his body hair through laser surgery. Throughout our marriage, he would often ingest my birth control pills, contending that they are a calming force for him. He also ingests female hormone pills which have caused him to develop breasts."

Karen told Dr. Cohen she was upset that Atwood "went so far" by including cross-dressing in her affidavit, and was worried that it would hurt him.

"[She] still feels protective of him," noted Dr. Cohen. "Discussed the protection of him as part of system that kept her in bondage."

At a court hearing the same day, which extended the restraining order, Sharpe finally turned up in court, setting eyes on Jacob Atwood for the first time. He glared at his nemesis throughout the hearing, later claiming that Atwood had berated him in a bathroom during a break.

"He told me, 'A fag transvestite like you shouldn't have children.' I just couldn't deal with any of it," Sharpe would testify. Atwood later denied that the confrontation ever took place.

But the following day, the attorney filed a motion requesting Dr. Sharpe be ordered by the court to be examined by a psychiatrist because of his recent "bizarre, abusive and vindictive conduct." Citing his dependency on alcohol and addiction to prescription medications, Atwood suggested the psychiatric exam should focus on the doctor's "anger management skills, his parenting skills, and his ability to deal with the children and stress generally."

Chapter Thirteen

DRESSED TO KILL

Throughout June, Karen Sharpe searched for a new man who could help her through her continuing tribulations. Although she was putting on a brave face to family and friends, Karen was distraught that her relationship with Marc Beauregard was falling apart. Initially, according to Connie Behnke, one of the few people she confided in, he had told her that he was divorced, but then she discovered he still had a wife and family and was seeing Karen on the side.

"That was really like the last thing she needed," said Behnke. "I just wanted so much for her to have a relationship with a really normal person who valued her. And he was actually just another guy who was abusive in another way."

She went on a date with another man, but was heartbroken when he told her he wasn't interested in a relationship because of her two young children, referring to them as "baggage."

She was still seeing Beauregard, who had a granddaughter, but she realized the only way they could be together was if he left his wife and fully committed to her.

"[She is] upset [that her] relationship isn't working out," wrote Dr. Cohen after their June 14 session. "Feels no one will want her."

The psychiatrist was building up Karen's self-esteem by using Richard Sharpe's cruelty as a metaphor for "brainwashing," and trying to make her forgive herself for remaining in the marriage for so long.

Five days later he wrote that Karen "needs to protect her boundaries" and that she was "hungry for an affirmation." She told him further tales of Sharpe's abuse while they were at Shelton High School in an almost "matter-of-fact" way.

"[Her] focus is on protecting her kids from this," read his case notes for June 19. "Believes Shannon knows something, doesn't know how much."

A week later, she would tell her psychiatrist, Beauregard betrayed her after going away on a trip with his wife and then lying to Karen about it. Although she had now resigned herself to the fact that she had no future with him, this seemed to make her stronger. Perhaps the one positive thing about the doomed affair was that it focused her on something other than Richard Sharpe.

But while his wife was struggling to find her own identity away from him, Dr. Sharpe was conducting business as usual. Despite his extra-curricular activities, following her constantly and staking out Hull Street, he and Shannon were now busy trying to consolidate his hair removal business and take it to the next level.

Soon after firing Brown, he put out the word that he needed a replacement, and began conducting interviews at his office at Great Ledge Lane. A young woman named Patricia Duffey heard about the LaseHair consulting job in her gym from a friend of Sharpe's. She then called Sharpe and went along for the interview, finding her prospective new boss heavily medicated on painkillers and other drugs.

"We talked about my background and the needs for the company," she remembered. "He was in a lot of pain and seemed to be focusing in and out of the conversation. [At one point] he closed his eyes and fell asleep."

Nevertheless, Duffey was most impressed with Dr. Sharpe's ambitious plans to take LaseHair national and thought he was "brilliant," accepting the job to run the company's day-to-day operations.

Duffey immediately began work, drawing up a plan to reorganize the company. She recommended he fire some of his staff and hire new employees. But during their business meetings Sharpe kept stalling on a final decision, saying he would have to refer the matter to his newly appointed president, Rich Fonte.

"He was in a lot of pain," remembered Duffey. "But we had started discussions."

Although Jacqui Feeney was no longer working for him, she and Scott Kilman were regular visitors to the impromptu evening parties he was now holding in the solarium/Jacuzzi at the rear of Great Ledge Lane. Dr. Sharpe would often be drugged up on painkillers and drunk on wine. He also smoked marijuana for an extra high.

"You know, I actually liked him when he was fucked up," said Kilman. "He had that solarium, and we used to go there to party with him and Paula."

Sharpe would put his favorite Beatles and Elton John CDs on the stereo and then turn the volume full-up.

"We would get pretty trashed," said Kilman. "It would be kind of late and he'd be blaring the music and just sitting back in his chair, just digging it—totally cooked out of his mind."

One night Paula Hiltz took Feeney to one side, complaining that Dr. Sharpe was impotent and wouldn't sleep with her. She said she was so frustrated lying next to him in bed at night without having sex, that she had started sleeping in a separate bedroom.

"I don't think he could have sex at that point because he was getting too into his tranquilizers," said Jacqui. "He told me that there was something wrong with him after his fall, and air was coming out of his penis."

When she had asked if Paula knew about his crossdressing, Sharpe became angry, saying that his new girlfriend didn't have a clue and he did not want her to find out.

Late one afternoon toward the end of June, Alden Tarr Jr. arrived at Great Ledge Lane to collect his son Audie, who had spent the day with his mother, Paula Hiltz. Usually the heavy-set, bushy-mustached welder with the gray crew-cut would wait outside the house for his son to come out, but today Dr. Richard Sharpe invited him in.

"He told me he needed some welding done," said Tarr. "I said I was awful busy and couldn't get to it."

Then Sharpe casually remarked that Paula had mentioned he was a gun collector and was selling off some firearms.

"He said he would like to buy a shotgun or a rifle for home protection," Tarr would later testify. "I told him I didn't have any for sale."

Sharpe let the matter drop and Tarr thought no more of it, driving Audie back to a second home on the other side of Gloucester, where he spent the summer.

On Sunday, July 2, Karen drove the children to the last family reunion the Hatfields would ever have at her sister's home in Beacon Falls, Connecticut. It was a beautiful weekend and Karen seemed happier and more relaxed than she'd ever been. It was as if she'd finally shaken the nightmare of Richard Sharpe, reclaiming her life with Mikey and Ali.

She and her brother Jamie, who had always been close, spent many hours talking that day about their lives and hopes for the future. He had also gone through a difficult divorce a few years earlier, and had been trying to guide Karen through hers. But she had always pushed him and other family members away, not wanting to reveal the true horror of what was going on. She feared they might get involved and upset her estranged husband, and he would carry out his threat to kill them.

"She was always very private with us," remembered Jamie, who had last seen his sister a couple of weeks earlier at a party he'd thrown at his house in East Providence, Rhode Island. "I wanted to go to court with her, but she was like, 'No, I need you to stay away. I've got everything under control.' She didn't want to let anybody know what was going on. And then I find out afterwards that he was threatening to kill me."

Three months of court appearances and Sharpe's harassment had taken a terrible toll on Karen, who told her sister Kathleen that she was ready to walk away and let Sharpe have everything.

"The whole divorce proceedings were very, very draining for her," remembered Kathleen. "She'd say it was going to go on forever and it was hard for her not to see the end."

Karen was particularly concerned about a legal proceeding scheduled in a couple of weeks' time, when Jacob Atwood would personally depose Dr. Sharpe in his law offices.

"It was just going to get really dirty and really ugly,"

Richard Sharpe's Shelton High School picture in the 1973 Argus Year Book (Shelton High School)

17-year-old Karen Hatfield had fallen under the spell of Shelton classmate Richard Sharpe by the time her picture appeared in the 1973 Argus Year Book (Shelton High School)

When Richard Sharpe was crowned the high school Prom King in 1973, Karen was already pregnant with their child and his official queen was a far plainer girl (Shelton High School)

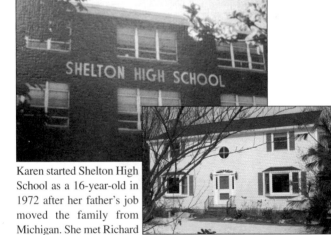

Karen started Shelton High School as a 16-year-old in 1972 after her father's job moved the family from Michigan. She met Richard soon after starting school (Shelton High School)

The Sharpes' house in Great Ledge Lane, Gloucester, where Dr. Sharpe would make millions of dollars as a cosmetic surgeon (John Glatt)

Dr. Richard Sharpe had a passion dressing in women's clothes from the time he was a little boy (Salem Probate Court Records)

The doctor liked to embrace the sluttish look during the frequent times he cross-dressed (Salem Probate Court Records)

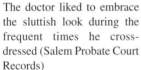

After his arrest for Karen's murder, Dr. Sharpe's daughter Shannon would place pictures of her father in drag into court records, to prevent him having access to his two younger children (Salem Probate Court Records)

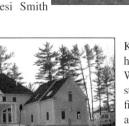

Karen was the perfect mother to her beloved baby daughter Ali (Desi Smith Photography)

Karen Hatfield and her family during a happy family occasion pictured in the garden at Great Ledge Lane several years before the murder. *Left to right*: Shannon, John Hatfield Sr., Karen, Ali, Patricia Hatfield and Mikey. (Desi Smith Photography)

Karen's $535,000 dream house at 19 Hull Street in Wenham gave her the strength and confidence to finally leave her long-time abuser husband (John Glatt)

The Sharpes' beautiful daughter Shannon worked for her father in his successful beauty business and helped build it into a multi-million-dollar enterprise (*The Boston Herald*)

The Blackburn Tavern in Gloucester, where Dr. Sharpe went drinking and dancing with his girl-friend Paula Hiltz just hours before the murder (John Glatt)

Dr. Sharpe walked up the football field–length driveway to the front doors of the Wenham house with a loaded rifle to kill his wife Karen (John Glatt)

The Black Toyota SUV in which he fled the scene of the crime to go on the run for almost thirty hours (Lawrence Superior Court Records)

19 Hull Street became a ghoulish attraction in the days after Karen's murder (John Glatt)

The crime scene in Wenham the day after the fatal killing (Lawrence Superior Court Records)

Dr. Richard Sharpe soon after his capture at the Pine View Lodge in Melvin Village, New Hampshire (*The Boston Herald*)

Karen died of a single gunshot wound in the hallway of her new Wenham home (Lawrence Superior Court Records)

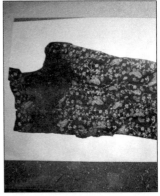

The blood-stained dress worn by Karen Sharpe when she died (Lawrence Superior Court Records)

Karen's divorce attorney, Jacob Atwood, who incurred the hatred of Dr. Sharpe in the weeks leading up to her murder (John Glatt)

The Hatfield-family legal team of Mark Smith, Jacob Atwood and Erin Shapiro at their Boston law offices (John Glatt)

Dr. Sharpe during an early court appearance at Salem Superior Court when he was charged with the murder of his wife (*The Boston Herald*)

For his murder trial in November of 2001, Richard Sharpe sported longer hair, keeping his eyes shut as if in pain throughout the proceedings. Prosecutors would accuse him of malingering (*The Boston Herald*)

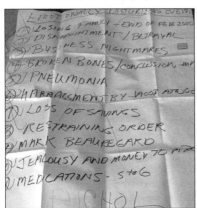

Defense attorney Juliane Balliro's eleven-point list of emotional distresses that had driven Sharpe to insanity (*The Boston Herald*)

Sharpe's furious outburst when he was not allowed to address Lawrence Superior Court, moments after he was sentenced to life in prison without parole
(*The Boston Herald*)

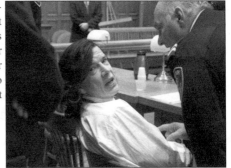

said Kathleen. "And Karen wasn't looking forward to any of that."

That Sunday, Kathleen took a photograph of her family at their happiest. The picture shows a radiant Karen with her brother John and their father, along with Mikey and Ali. It captures all the love and tenderness that surrounded the Hatfields, a poignant moment in time, never to be repeated.

"We had a wonderful, wonderful time that day," said Kathleen. "And that was the last time that I ever saw her."

That night Karen and the kids returned to Gloucester for the annual Horribles Parade. Every year without fail the Sharpes camped out at the same spot on Main Street, to watch the colorful July Fourth procession pass by, followed by a fireworks display. The 2000 theme was "The Little Mermaid," and Karen had brought a picnic lunch, arranging to meet all her friends for a sidewalk feast. Dressed in a beautiful new turquoise suit bought for the occasion, she prayed Richard wouldn't turn up and spoil it for them.

Earlier, Mikey and Ali had gone to Great Ledge Lane for a visitation, and their father had invited them to go and watch the fireworks with him.

"Michael said he was going with Mom," remembered Dr. Sharpe. "I just sort of showed up."

Karen Beswick was watching the floats go by with Karen and her children, when Sharpe suddenly appeared out of nowhere, trying to put his arm around his estranged wife. Karen froze and tried to push him away, telling her friend right in front of him, "This is not what you're thinking."

Embarrassed and afraid for Karen that Dr. Sharpe would cause a big scene in front of Steve and Carol

Figurido and Cynthia and Mike Goodhew, Beswick attempted to lighten things up, asking little Ali about her summer.

"Then she said to me, 'Children are supposed to have fun, aren't they?' " remembered the headmistress. "And I said, 'Yes, that's what summer's all about. Children are supposed to have a really good time.' "

Breaking into the conversation, Richard Sharpe declared, "Well, yes, we're trying, but the children don't seem to have fun."

Beswick found this a "strange, strange comment," and carried on talking to Karen about her and the kids' plans for the summer. As Karen went across Main Street to chat with friends, promising to call her later, and reiterating that appearances were deceptive, Sharpe put his arm around her to guide her, and once again she pushed him away. Steve Figurido, who knew all about the restraining order, saw Karen's discomfort and ordered Sharpe to leave her alone. Looking hurt, Richard sat down a few feet away from his family, watching the parade without another word.

"There's a big group of about fifty men who walk in the parade [to highlight] violence against women," said Karen Beswick. "I watched them pass by him and I remember looking over to him and wondering what he must be thinking. But he had a completely blank look on his face."

On Wednesday, July 12, Rich Fonte flew up from Florida for two days of business meetings with Dr. Sharpe about the future of LaseHair. The middle-aged former Timex executive arrived at Great Ledge Lane with a new business plan to help the company regroup and get back on its feet. Fonte presented the plan to Dr. Sharpe and Patricia Duffey, and on Thursday afternoon they adjourned to a Gloucester restaurant to continue their talks.

"We were talking a lot about the future of the business," remembered Duffey, who was now running day-to-day operations. "About our plans to grow."

At one point during the luncheon, Sharpe began to stare straight at her blankly, making her frightened.

"He actually seemed to lose his focus," she said. "We were having a conversation about the future of the company and all of a sudden he stopped and there was this cold stare for a period of time."

Then, just as suddenly, he refocused on the business conversation, as if nothing had happened. After the meal, Duffey told her family about how eerie it had been, resolving never to be alone with her boss again.

Later that day, Dr. Sharpe took Shannon, Rich Fonte and Paula Hiltz to a nearby Italian restaurant called the Chianti Cafe & Grill for dinner. Again they spoke business and Shannon reported on her recent trip to Asia to scout out new LaseHair opportunities. In two days' time she was due to move to Manhattan with her fiancé Wayne Cohen, a second-year law student. They planned to move into an apartment together and were scheduled to sign the lease on Saturday.

At one point during dinner, Sharpe asked Fonte the best way to transfer large amounts of money abroad to tax-free havens like the Cayman Islands.

"[Rich] was very intrigued," said Fonte. "He wanted to know how it was happening."

Chapter Fourteen

PRELUDE TO A MURDER

Karen Sharpe arrived at Connie Behnke's house in Essex, at 8:30 a.m. on Friday, July 14, to pick up Ellie and Natalie Behnke for a three-and-a-half-hour play date with Mikey and Ali at Great Ledge Lane. It was a cool, cloudy morning with temperatures in the sixties, as Karen drove the four young children to her former home in Gloucester. After leaving the kids, Karen went shopping to buy a new set of clothes for her long-anticipated cruise around Gloucester Harbor that night.

As usual Mikey and Ali were reluctant to spend the morning with their father, never knowing what mood he would be in. But lately he had changed, desperately trying to prove to Karen that he could be the perfect father.

"For the last few weeks my kids were saying they couldn't believe how he was making these healthy lunches of pasta and broccoli," remembered Connie Behnke. "He was still trying to win her back."

Two days earlier, Karen had joyously told Dr. Cohen that she had noticed a positive change in her husband's attitude towards her. Misreading his signals, she now believed he had finally resigned himself to losing her, and was moving on.

"She felt something new," Dr. Cohen duly noted. "That he was giving up, letting go of her. Incredible feeling of relief and freedom. Possibility of new beginning with the kids. Not feeling so desperate to be with a man. Maybe this will all work out. Best she has felt in 27 years."

The four children arrived to find Dr. Sharpe immersed in a business meeting with Rich Fonte. Paula Hiltz and her niece Holly, who had recently been hired as a nurse, were busy working in the basement office.

Feeling ignored by the adults, they played with each other in the living room and on an outdoor trampoline. But they soon got bored and nine-year-old Natalie Behnke started calling her mother, complaining that Sharpe was busy working and making phone calls, and they all wanted to come home.

"They called a lot and I was really concerned," Connie remembered. "Usually they don't call me at all."

Several times Dr. Sharpe came on the phone to placate Behnke, who was becoming increasingly worried that something was wrong. He told her that once he had finished work, he would take all the kids to McDonald's for burgers, and then to Curious Creatures, a local pet shop.

The children were now antsy, playing games of hide-and-seek around the LaseHair office. Throughout the meeting to discuss making Patricia Duffey the new president of Lasehair, they had to stop while Sharpe shooed the children upstairs.

Then, leaving the kids with Duffey and his nurse, Dr. Sharpe and Fonte left for a bank in downtown Gloucester. Previously, on his boss's instructions, Fonte had inflated his $3,000 invoice for his consultation services to

$7,000. Desperate to disguise his net worth, Sharpe would pocket the extra $4,000 in cash, fearing a probate court-ordered deposition the following week in Jacob Atwood's office. This way it would not be placed in escrow until a final divorce settlement was reached. Fonte had agreed to the subterfuge and they both went to the bank where the LaseHair check was cashed, with Sharpe taking the extra amount. Then they returned to Great Ledge Lane where Sharpe called his brother, in the first of three calls that day, to check on the status of a sophisticated new Pentium 38700 computer server with a SCSI Hard Drive that Bob was building and planned to install in the office the following week.

"He was calling me," remembered Bob. " 'Can you put this in? Can you put that in?' "

At around noon, Fonte left to spend the weekend with his family in Connecticut, and Sharpe took the children to Curious Creatures and McDonald's. A couple of hours later they returned to Great Ledge Lane, where Karen picked up the kids to drop them off at their respective homes.

Dr. Sharpe then made a series of phone calls. First, he telephoned his brother again with some fresh instructions about the computer server. Next he called a local florist, ordering a dozen red roses to be sent to Karen in Wenham. Finally, he called Connie Behnke, asking if she could arrange a date for him with Karen, saying he was desperate for a reconciliation.

"I said there's no way that will ever happen," she remembered. "I told him Karen had moved on and started a new life, and that he should as well."

He then broke into "an angry tirade," accusing Karen of stealing all his money and how he hated Jacob Atwood, who was responsible for everything that had happened. When she put down the phone, Connie shook her head in disbelief, amazed at how he appeared to place his fortune so far above Karen's love.

Prosecutors would allege that at this point Dr. Sharpe, who had heard that Karen would be attending a cruise that night with friends, began putting his murderous plan into action. Realizing he would be the prime suspect from the outset, he decided to murder his wife in front of witnesses. Indeed, say prosecutors, he had spent weeks carefully laying the foundations for a later insanity plea—even before pulling the trigger.

Richard Sharpe had spent his whole life outsmarting the world to become rich and famous in his chosen medical field, so he didn't consider that the police would present too big an obstacle for someone of his genius.

At about 5:00 p.m. Sharpe invited Paula Hiltz to join him for dinner. He had wanted to go to Tom Sheas Seafood Restaurant in Essex, but Paula persuaded him instead to go to Halibut Point in downtown Gloucester. She needed to get a prescription filled at a drug store before her health insurance ran out. She also wanted to close some windows she had left open earlier that day during a visit to Alden Tarr's with their son. Sharpe reluctantly agreed, saying he too had to stop off at his practice, which was right behind Osco Drug. Just before he left, Sharpe went to the bathroom where he took six different painkillers and tranquilizers to steady himself for what he had to do.

Sharpe drove Hiltz the short journey towards the harbor, where he let her off at Osco on Eastern Avenue. Prosecutors believe he then went to his practice where he collected a .22-caliber rifle he had hidden there earlier. Where he got the gun remains a mystery to this day.

They met up again at about 7:00 p.m. at Halibut Point on Main Street, taking a table underneath an antique maritime clock. It was a busy Friday night at the boozy seafood restaurant where sailors rub shoulders with local businessmen. It is a friendly place where everyone knows everyone, and throughout the meal Paula was chatting and table-hopping with old friends.

Dr. Sharpe seemed distracted as he ate his haddock and downed six or seven glasses of merlot. A little after 9:00 p.m., Sharpe called his brother Bob in Shelton again, to arrange for the delivery of the new server. Bob had just started watching a movie on television and agreed to call their brother Ben, to make arrangements to deliver the computer hardware to Gloucester the following Friday.

Straight after the call, Dr. Sharpe paid the check and seemed in a good mood with the effects of the wine and pills. He suggested they go to the Blackburn Tavern, insisting on driving the half-mile to the bar at the corner of Washington and Main Streets, saying that Paula could drive home from there. A rock band had already started a set by the time they arrived, and Sharpe went to the bar, ordering another merlot and a Killian's Red for Paula. Then they danced together to the live music, before Paula returned to the bar to get another round, this time insisting that Richard drink a Diet Coke to sober up.

At about 10:00 p.m. they left the Blackburn Tavern and Hiltz drove to Alden Tarr's house, a few blocks away at 108 Washington Street. She pulled into the narrow driveway and said she would just run in and close the windows. She told Sharpe to wait in the Toyota 4Runner.

"He started to get out of the car," she remembered. "I said, 'Rich, you can't come in here.'"

Refusing to take no for an answer, Sharpe walked towards the house anyway, saying he wanted to see a coffee table Paula had promised him for the office. Eventually she backed down and allowed him to come into Tarr's house, thinking, "What's the harm?"

He followed up onto the porch and through the front door, turning right into the dining room, where she closed two windows. Sharpe took another right into the darkened living room, which was only half-lit from the hallway.

There was still enough light for him to see Alden Tarr's gun collection, hanging from a gun rack on the far wall above a grand piano. He walked to the rack and reached over, taking a .30-caliber Weatherby Mark Deluxe hunting rifle. As he grabbed it, he stepped on some of little Audie's toys.

"I heard a noise like him tripping," said Hiltz. "I said, 'Are you all right?' and he said, 'Yes.' "

Dr. Sharpe would later claim he also took a handful of bullets that were lying nearby, although both Hiltz and Tarr would maintain that the only ammunition in the house was securely locked up in a gun safe, in a closet off the bedroom.

Then, as Paula was closing the windows, Sharpe sneaked out of the house with the rifle, throwing it in the back seat of his SUV. When Paula came out of the house she was horrified to see her boyfriend urinating on the sidewalk.

"I said, 'What are you doing?' " she would later testify. "And he said he had to go to the bathroom."

She grabbed him by the arm, telling him there were two bathrooms in the house he could use. They then went back inside and Sharpe relieved himself in the downstairs facility.

"He was a little shaky on his feet," she said. "And I stood by the door."

Then they both went upstairs to look at the coffee

table she was giving him. Sharpe went back downstairs and she heard the front door slam shut. He came out to see Alden Tarr's neighbor, Michelle Trioli, sitting outside her house, staring up at the clear black skies at a perfect full moon.

"He was acting kind of odd," remembered Trioli. "It was a gorgeous night and he asked me if I was sunbathing, telling me how it wasn't good for my skin or complexion."

Paula overheard him and told him he was being silly, saying she was only catching the rays of the moon. Then they left without another word for the short drive back to Great Ledge Lane.

It was 10:45 p.m. when they arrived at the house. Before going in they stood outside for a moment looking at the stars. Dr. Sharpe seemed in great spirits as they went straight up to his solarium/Jacuzzi and he put a Beatles CD on the stereo. Suddenly he announced that he had mislaid his pager, saying it must have slipped off his belt while they were at Halibut Point, and needed it urgently, as he often received 911 call-outs for medical emergencies. Paula called the restaurant, but they had not found it.

She left to look for it at Alden Tarr's house, saying she would spend the night there, and promising to telephone Richard the minute she found it. As soon as he heard her drive away, Sharpe dialed Karen's cell phone, as he had done at least a half-a-dozen times that evening. When there was no answer yet again, he tried to clear his head for his trip to Wenham. When he felt composed enough, he turned off the stereo and walked downstairs to get the rifle he had picked up from his practice earlier that night. He loaded it and unlocked the safety catch, making sure it was ready to fire.

Then he put a brown leather jacket on over his white dress shirt and black jeans and set off for the seven-mile drive to Wenham.

It had been a wonderful night for Karen Sharpe, more than fulfilling her expectations for her "coming-out party." As she had danced the night away with her friends, the chains of her twenty-seven years of imprisonment with Richard Sharpe seemed to fall from her shoulders, and she felt as though anything was possible.

She arrived home at 19 Hull Street at about 11:20 p.m. with her brother Jamie and his girlfriend Christine Regan, bursting to tell Mikey and Ali about her fabulous evening. It seemed symbolic of the beginning of her new life, where she wouldn't have to live in fear and be looking over her shoulder all the time.

And as she prepared to take her babysitter Kristen Dormitzer to the hospital to treat her eye, which had been accidentally scratched by little Aurora Regan, Karen felt the dark clouds of her old life parting, revealing a new radiant sunshine and clear blue skies.

Chapter Fifteen

"I HEARD THE GUN GO OFF"

At 11:30 p.m. Dr. Richard Sharpe climbed in his black Toyota SUV, turned on the headlights and set off from 8 Great Ledge Lane. On the back seat lay his loaded .22-caliber rifle and the Weatherby shotgun he had stolen earlier from Alden Tarr's house. His raging anger over what he perceived as Karen's treachery neutralized the alcohol and drugs he'd taken. He felt a rush of adrenaline as he began crossing a line from which he could never return.

Glancing up at the full moon peering through scattered clouds, he carefully negotiated the narrow winding road from the house, driving over the single-lane bridge. He then turned right onto Sumner Street until he came to Route 133, also known as Essex Avenue. He had made the seven-and-a-half-mile journey numerous times, in so many different states of mind, that he could practically drive it with his eyes closed.

There was no traffic in sight as he turned left, gunning the powerful SUV a mile to the Exit 14 ramp of Route 128. He then headed southwest towards Boston, hitting the accelerator hard as he flew past the School Street and Pine Street exits, finally getting off at Exit 17, towards Beverly Farms. He turned right at the fork in the ramp onto Grapevine Road, driving past Gordon College, which was bathed in moonlight.

Then, just ten minutes after he had left West Gloucester, he slowed down, turning left onto Hull Street and parking at the end of the long driveway to Karen's house.

Turning off his headlights, he got out of the car, reaching into the back seat for the heavy loaded rifle, and closing the door as softly as possible. Then he walked up the football field–length driveway toward the house. He could see lights in the windows of the lavish two-story colonial, and hear voices.

All the anger and resentment over what Karen had done to him welled up inside his stomach with each step towards the house. She had to die for the crimes of taking his money and his children, and daring to leave him. Even now, as he approached her house gripping a loaded rifle, he loved her more than anything in his miserable world. But it was a twisted love. Not love in the normal sense of the word. He knew he had to destroy both of their lives, as it was far better for her to be dead than to live a life apart from him.

Now, resting the rifle by the double front doors on the porch, he pushed one open. He poked his head inside and his eyes adjusted to the brightly lit hallway. Then he saw a pretty blonde woman, whom he had never met before, holding a bandage to her eye.

"Where's Karen? I need to talk to Karen," he said softly, almost in a whisper. The room was now quiet, as Sharpe recognized his brother-in-law Jamie and his girlfriend. Then Karen walked towards him until she was just a few feet away.

"Richard, you're not supposed to be here," she said

sternly, their eyes meeting for a split second, as she tried
to shoo him out of the house. In her hand she was holding the piece of paper she'd written Kristen Dormitzer's
health insurance information on, but Sharpe mistook it
for the restraining order against him.

Then Karen recognized that familiar and terrible look
on her husband's face, and felt a chill as he kicked the
door open wider, revealing the cocked rifle, aimed
straight at her heart.

"Oh my God!" she screamed, as she turned to run
away. Then, without another word he pulled the trigger,
sending a .22-caliber bullet at point-blank range straight
through her back, ripping into her lungs and severing
her spinal cord, before coming out of her chest. There
was a deafening explosion and a heat flash, waking up
little Mikey and Ali who were asleep in the nearby television room.

Dr. Richard Sharpe then calmly walked back down
the long drive to his Toyota #4Runner, turned on the
headlights, started the engine and sped off into the night.

In the minutes after he fled, there was fear and chaos,
as the shocked eyewitnesses to Karen's slaughter fully
expected Dr. Sharpe to return and massacre them too.
Kristen Dormitzer, who had been so close to the rifle
that she had felt the heat flash when it went off, had
dived for cover and then run across the foyer to the
television room to save the three young children. Fearing
for all their lives, she hid with them behind a couch in
the living room, as she dialed 911 on her cell phone.

"But it didn't work," she remembered. "It just rang
and rang and rang."

Unsure if Sharpe was still waiting outside the house,
she looked out a window, but there was no sign of him.
Then she bundled the frightened children down the hall-

way into a bathroom shower, where they huddled together until the police came.

Shocked and stunned from seeing his beloved sister gunned down in cold blood, Jamie Hatfield made some fast decisions. Initially he had rushed out of the open double door after his brother-in-law, but then stopped in his tracks, swung around and slammed the door shut, deadbolting it.

"Then I went to try and save my sister," he remembered. "I was afraid that more people were going to get shot."

As he cradled his dying sister's blood-soaked head in his arms, he screamed for the cell phone that was in his overnight bag, lying nearby.

Then he and his girlfriend Christine both dialed 911 separately, to summon help.

"There's been a shooting!" he sobbed to the emergency dispatcher at Wenham Police Department, who clocked the call at 11:52 a.m. "My sister's been shot. We need emergency people here, and we need officers. The best you have."

When the dispatcher asked who had shot Karen, Jamie replied: "Dr. Richard Sharpe's the shooter," explaining that he was outside and armed and could return at any moment and kill more people.

The dispatcher tried to calm him down, assuring him that police were on their way to Hull Street and asking where Karen had been shot.

"I don't know where she's been shot," Jamie screamed in frustration. "It doesn't matter right now. I don't know what he was driving. It was maybe a Toyota. Possibly a Toyota. Who knows what he's driving! He's not in the house. He's outside the fucking house! He is outside the house!"

After he put down the phone and was still holding

Karen in his arms, Jamie looked up and saw little Mikey.

"[He] was standing in the foyer staring at Karen, whose eyes were rolled back in her head," he later remembered. "Michael was crying uncontrollably during this period."

Then Mikey asked him if his father had shot his mother, and his uncle had no alternative but to tell him the truth.

"Why did my father shoot my mother?" sobbed the little boy as he stared down at Karen's lifeless body in a growing pool of blood. "Why did he do that? I never want to see my father again."

The five minutes it took the paramedics to arrive seemed like "an eternity" to Jamie, as he cradled his dying sister and tried to comfort Mikey.

When the police finally did come, they cordoned off the house and began searching the grounds for Dr. Sharpe, summoning back-up, saying he was armed and dangerous. Ambulances arrived to take Karen's body to Beverly Hospital. Curious neighbors, who had been awakened by the gunshot, came out to see what was happening. Police ordered them back into their houses and told them to lock their doors.

David Sabatini was in bed when he heard a loud bang, followed by a door slamming. He went to his second-floor bedroom window, which directly faces Karen's house, just in time to see Richard Sharpe walking briskly away from the house.

"I followed him from one window to another window, all the way to the end of the driveway," Sabatini would later remember. "Then I saw a car door light go on and the headlights. Then the car backed up and sped off."

The Wenham police, who had not had to deal with a murder for almost twenty years, set up a crime scene and did their best to handle the situation. But their back-up from nearby Beverly was late in arriving, due to the dispatcher at the Hamilton–Wenham Emergency Center failing to realize that there was a second Hull Street in Beverly. Instead of heading for Wenham, a squad of Beverly police officers had duly gone to the wrong 19 Hull Street, ordering an innocent 14-year-old boy out of the house at gunpoint, and blocked off the whole street before realizing their mistake. The frightened teenager was later released and embarrassed police would later refuse to comment on their mistake to the press.

Shannon Sharpe got the cell phone call from Jamie at about midnight. She had left Hull Street just before her mother had returned from the cruise to drive to Boston's South Street Station to pick up Wayne Cohen, who was arriving from New York on a late train.

"Shannon," said Jamie, as calmly as he could, without mentioning that Karen was already dead, "your father just shot your mother."

Shannon screamed and had to be calmed down by passers-by. Then Wayne arrived and took her to Beverly Hospital, where doctors had pronounced Karen dead on arrival. When Shannon arrived her mother's body was on its way to the morgue, to be laid out for an autopsy.

Shannon and Wayne were ushered into a small office and told that Karen was dead.

It was well after midnight when Jamie called his sister Kathleen Lembo to give her the news. Kathleen and her husband Victor were preparing for bed when the phone rang. She immediately worried that something was wrong, as no one ever called that late.

"I didn't know who else to call," said Jamie, sounding frantic, but under control. "I can't deal with anybody else right now."

Kathleen asked him what was going on and he tearfully told her that all Karen's fears about Sharpe had been realized.

"He's shot her," he stammered.

"You must be kidding," said Kathleen in disbelief. "Is she OK?"

Trying to protect his sister from the awful truth, Jamie merely said that Karen had been shot in the arm by Richard. She then asked where Shannon was, and Jamie said she was OK, adding that the police were now looking for Sharpe. Then he put down the phone, saying that he had to talk to the state police.

Believing her sister's injury was non–life-threatening, Kathleen called her brother John and they decided they must tell their parents and then have the family evacuate their various houses, as Dr. Sharpe was still on the loose and knew where they all lived.

"We knew we had to tell my parents, but we didn't want to tell them over the phone," said Kathleen. "We were really convinced that [Rich] was going to head down here."

After arranging for her own two children to stay at a safe-house, Kathleen and Victor made the twenty-minute drive to Shelton to meet John at their parents' house. By this time Shannon had called her aunt from Beverly Hospital, tearfully breaking the news that Karen had died.

"It was just incredible. Incredible," Kathleen would later remember.

At 3:20 on Sunday morning John Hatfield called his father on his cell phone from the driveway outside his parents' house, with Kathleen by his side for moral support.

"He asked me to come down and open the door," said Karen's father. "And I knew there had to be something very wrong."

Without telling his wife, he went downstairs to find

his son and daughter standing by the front door. They insisted he come back inside, and Kathleen went upstairs to tell her mother, while John told his father to sit down in the living room, where he broke the news of Karen's murder.

In stunned disbelief Hatfield went upstairs to comfort his wife, but there was little time to mourn that night, as the police wanted them to leave their house immediately, in case Richard Sharpe paid a visit.

Shannon Sharpe remained at the hospital, calling friends and making arrangements to keep her young brother and sister safe. At first they were taken over the road to the Sabatinis' house, where Shannon and Wayne later joined them.

As soon as Connie Behnke got the call from Shannon Sharpe, in the early hours of Saturday morning, she and her husband Jim went straight to the Sabatinis' to look after Mikey and Ali.

The Behnkes had been asleep when the phone rang and they hadn't answered at first. But as it kept ringing, Jim picked it up.

"Oh my God, Connie," he blurted out to his wife. "It's Shannon at the hospital. Rich shot Karen."

They immediately got dressed and drove to Beverly Hospital, still thinking Karen had only been slightly injured.

"It was the strangest thing," remembered Connie. "I was kind of excited on the way to the hospital, because Shannon had only told Jim she had been shot. And I'm thinking, This is perfect. She's going to have her arm in a sling, but he's going to be put away for attempted murder. It never occurred to me [she was dead]."

But when the Behnkes arrived at the hospital, they ran into Wayne Cohen, who told them Karen was gone.

"It was a shock," said Connie, tearfully. "So hard. And from then it was a blur."

The Behnkes volunteered to go to the Sabatinis' to help look after Mikey and Ali. Connie spent the rest of the night trying to calm them down as best she could.

"Michael was really frightened when he woke up the next day," she remembered. "He definitely knew something horrible had happened. But I remember Ali asked if Mommy's toe was better. It was one of those really sweet things."

The following morning, detectives ordered everyone to leave Hull Street and check into a nearby hotel, as they could no longer guarantee their safety. Although police all over the northeast had joined in the manhunt for Dr. Sharpe, it was as if he had disappeared into thin air.

Chapter Sixteen

MANHUNT

At about one o'clock on Sunday morning, Sergeant Michael Cronin of the Massachusetts State Police Detective Unit arrived at 19 Hull Street to head the investigation into Karen's murder. He put out an all points bulletin for Dr. Sharpe, warning he was armed and highly dangerous, either driving a Toyota #4Runner, license plate #H13131 or a 2000 Ford E-150 Custom Van, license #5168NH.

Working with Officer John Gray and Sergeant James Colt of the Wenham Police Department, Sergeant Cronin organized a crime scene, bringing in a team of highly trained forensic scientists to gather evidence. Early that morning police divers dragged the pond at the end of Karen's driveway in a fruitless search for weapons. The next day Sergeant Cronin interviewed Karen Sharpe's family and everyone who knew Dr. Sharpe, for any leads as to where he could be hiding out. Detectives believed that one of Dr. Sharpe's LaseHair business affiliates might be helping him.

Police also got warrants to search the Great Ledge Lane home and Dr. Sharpe's practice in the Cape Ann

Market Place on Eastern Avenue, Gloucester.

"Right now our main thrust is finding Dr. Sharpe," declared Wenham detective Lieutenant John Malone to local reporters. "He's out there and we believe he has the weapon."

Early Saturday morning, Paula Hiltz was interviewed by Massachusetts State Trooper Steve O'Connor at 108 Washington Street. She told him of her previous night with Richard Sharpe and opened up Alden Tarr's gun safe with her own set of keys. When Tarr arrived soon afterwards, he told detectives his Weatherby hunting rifle was missing from the gun rack. He also checked the gun safe, confirming that no ammunition had been taken.

Later that day Mikey and Ali were taken to stay in Newton, Massachusetts, where Wayne's mother, Dr. Sylvia Cohen, a child psychologist, was flying in from Scottsdale, Arizona, to provide grief counseling for the children.

"Nobody really knew where to go or how to handle the situation," Karen Beswick, who had been asked to attend the sessions, would later remember.

On Saturday morning, as the story of Karen Sharpe's brutal killing by her doctor husband exploded onto Massachusetts radio and television, there was still no sign of Dr. Richard Sharpe. Local and national reporters converged on Wenham en masse, interviewing anyone who had any knowledge of the Sharpe family. A multimillionaire Harvard M.D. who had killed his wife and was on the run—it had all the ingredients of a major news story, but at that time reporters had little idea just how big it would become.

Just two hours after the killing, *Gloucester Daily Times* photographer Desi Smith got a call from his news editor telling him there had been a murder in Wenham, and asking him to investigate. Smith threw on some clothes and drove to the Wenham police station where a couple of reporters were already there, waiting to be briefed.

When Smith found out that the victim was Karen Sharpe and the suspect her husband, whose house he had worked on eighteen months earlier, he was stunned.

"I nearly fell over," he remembered. "I was totally taken by surprise."

Along with the other reporters, Smith went to Great Ledge Lane, which a Massachusetts SWAT team had already cordoned off, thinking Dr. Sharpe might be hiding out there. He spent the rest of the day with the media posse, becoming part of the story himself, when he mentioned to a Boston TV crew that he knew the Sharpes and had pictures of a family gathering.

"All the other news stations jumped in with cameras and stuff," he remembered. "And all of a sudden I've got microphones in my face. I was very uncomfortable."

Still in shock from Karen's death, the Sabatinis, who had been on the cruise with her the night before, told the *Boston Herald* they were "sickened" by the murder.

"It's devastating; it's unfair," said an emotional Lane Sabatini. "He ruined a lot of lives last night. He didn't want to accept the divorce. She just didn't want him here."

Her friend and former Great Ledge Lane neighbor, Steve Figurido, who owned a variety store in Gloucester, said it was a "nightmare."

"The guy must have snapped," he said. "He was a workaholic. There's a lot of people who aren't going to take this very easily. They're crushed."

His wife Carol said Karen had only told friends "bits and pieces" about the extent of the abuse she suffered from her husband.

"Now it's all come together," she said. "Unfortunately it's too late for Karen."

On Saturday morning, a local radio station in Burlington, Massachusetts, carried the story of Karen's murder as its lead item. Dr. Richard Sharpe, who had switched on his car radio, heard that he had successfully killed Karen and was now being hunted for her murder.

After killing his wife, Dr. Sharpe had driven west along Route 128, towards Gloucester. He would later testify that he was "confused" as he stopped his black SUV by the side of the road between Wenham and Gloucester, throwing the Weatherby rifle and the ammunition out the window. He would always deny the existence of a second .22 rifle, although ballistic experts would later say it was impossible to fire the .22-caliber bullet which had killed Karen Sharpe from the larger-barreled .30-caliber Weatherby.

"I simply dropped [the rifle] out of the window," he would claim, although a thorough search of that stretch of busy two-lane road would fail to find anything. "It was something I didn't want."

Then, according to Dr. Sharpe, he turned around and headed east along 128, driving thirty-five miles to Burlington, Massachusetts. The road was almost deserted at that time of night and he finally stopped in a parking area, curled up and went to sleep.

On Saturday morning he woke up and heard that police were hunting him for the murder of Karen.

"[It said] that there was a shooting in Wenham and they wanted to talk to me," he later testified. "I knew something had happened, but I was confused. I didn't know what I had done until then."

He then decided to keep to the back roads to avoid detection, heading north on Route 3 from Burlington towards New Hampshire. Tuning in the car radio to one of his favorite oldies stations, he followed Route 3 over the New Hampshire border through Nashua and Hooksett, to Concord and Franklin, before stopping at a gas station. He filled up the SUV and bought a bottle of Gatorade, using his own credit card, as he only had sixty dollars in cash. Later, prosecutors would claim that deliberately using his credit card was just one more ploy to appear insane.

It was a comfortable summer afternoon in the low 80s as he slowly drove up Route 3 through Laconia, before turning west at Meredith into the rural Hampshire countryside. Later he would claim he had suicide on his mind, after learning he had killed Karen.

It was early evening when he stopped at a small variety store, buying a six-pack of Labatt beer and a length of clothesline, which he intended to use to hang himself.

"I thought it would be less painful if I was drinking," he would explain.

At about 8:15 p.m. he pulled into 19 Mile Bay Cottages, a small motel in Tuftonboro, one hundred miles north of Boston. The owner's son Chuck DeLorio was in the driveway with his wife Eileen, chatting to guests, when Sharpe's brand new Toyota SUV pulled in off Route 109 and onto the circular driveway.

The DeLorios walked up to the van and immediately thought there was something odd about the puffy-eyed, "chalky" white–faced driver, wearing a stiff, white dress shirt in a vacation spot in the middle of summer.

"It looked like he had been crying and hadn't slept for days," remembered DeLorio. "He was fumbling with the window control, but finally rolled down the window and asked in a soft voice if I had any rooms for the night. I told him we didn't, as we don't take overnight guests."

Then DeLorio suggested he try the Pine View Lodge a few miles east on Route 109 in Melvin Village. Dr. Sharpe thanked him and then drove off without another word.

"Geez, that guy gives me the creeps," he told his wife, noting that the SUV had Massachusetts license plates. She agreed, saying he was "weird," and "scary-looking."

A few minutes later Dr. Sharpe booked into room 12 at the Pine View Lodge, which lies on the edge of Lake Winnipesaukee, paying for it with his credit card. He registered under his own name, and then locked himself in the room and started drinking his six-pack of beer.

"I made a noose and looked around in the hotel for a place to set it up," he would testify. "But there wasn't any good place in the room."

Then he lay down on the bed and fell fast asleep.

That night Chuck DeLorio turned on the eleven o'clock WBZ-TV Boston news for the weather forecast, and was stunned by a segment about a rich Gloucester doctor who was on the run after murdering his wife.

"And I looked at his picture on the TV and I was speechless," said DeLorio. "I said, 'That's him! That's the guy who was in the driveway three hours ago.' I was flabbergasted."

By the time Eileen DeLorio came out of the bathroom the story was over, and for the next few minutes DeLorio wrestled with calling a special hotline police number that was given on the news. He then called his mother Ann DeLorio for advice, and she immediately telephoned the Tuftonboro Police Department with the tip.

Police Chief Andy Shagouri, who heads up the tiny two-man department, clocked the call at 11:14 p.m. and immediately went into action. He first checked with the Massachusetts State Police, who confirmed DeLorio's description of the fugitive and the van. Then he called the owner of the Pine View Lodge, who corroborated that a Richard Sharpe had checked in earlier and had been driving a black Toyota #4Runner.

"I called the New Hampshire State Police, who have a SWAT team," said Shagouri, "and arranged to meet the other officers in Melvin Village, well away from the motel."

Within minutes of the first call from Ann DeLorio, Sergeant Cronin was on his way to meet New Hampshire detectives at a command post, hastily set up at a small variety store in Melvin Village, half a mile away from the motel. As three units of the Massachusetts State Police, the SWAT team and the Wenham and Gloucester Police Departments, made their way to the variety store for a tactical meeting, Chief Shagouri drove to Pine View Lodge to get the lay of the land.

He parked some distance from the motel so he could quietly check on the #4Runner without being seen. Then he walked around the perimeter, noting that the room where Sharpe was hiding was the end one on the right, so other guests could be safely evacuated without arousing his suspicion.

At about 12:30 Sunday morning, Chief Shagouri briefed Sergeant Cronin and the SWAT team, and they decided to immediately put up roadblocks at either side of Pine View Lodge on Route 109 in case Dr. Sharpe tried to escape. Their biggest concern was that Dr. Sharpe might have a scoped rifle, and start shooting at police, or even make hostages of other guests.

Ninety minutes later the SWAT team began setting up observation posts around Dr. Sharpe's room, bringing in tear gas, halogen lights and other equipment they'd need to storm it. The Tuftonboro Fire Department's

EMC Unit also stood by, in case anyone needed medical attention.

"It was a little after two o'clock when we started evacuating [guests] and taking them to the Melvin Village Fire Station, which had been opened up as a shelter," said Shagouri. "It took about an hour until we had cleared the section of the motel where he was."

At about 3:30 a.m. the commander of the SWAT team gave the order to move in for the operation. At the given signal, officers smashed two windows of Sharpe's room and hurled in canisters of pepper spray, while other members of the team, wearing breathing apparatus, opened the door with a master key, ordering Sharpe out at gunpoint.

"He came staggering out without a fight or anything," said Chief Shagouri. "They asked him if there were any weapons in the room, and he said no."

Dr. Richard Sharpe was read his rights and arrested for Karen's murder at 3:51 a.m., exactly twenty-eight hours after the killing. His unusually pale face was red from the pepper-spray, and he kept his teary eyes tightly shut as he was escorted from the room through a gauntlet of bright lights into a police cruiser. Then he was driven to the Wolfeboro Police Department to be fingerprinted and taken into custody before being extradited back to Massachusetts.

After obtaining a search warrant from a judge, Sergeant Cronin searched Sharpe's hotel room, finding no weapons or ammunition. All that was there was a length of clothesline fashioned into a noose and an empty six-pack of Labatt's.

Chapter Seventeen

PICKING UP THE PIECES

On Sunday morning, Essex County District Attorney Kevin M. Burke held a press conference at his office in a small shopping mall in Salem, Massachusetts. He briefed reporters about Dr. Sharpe's arrest in Tuftonboro earlier that morning, expressing "shock" that the so-called brilliant medic had used his own name and vehicle when checking into the Pine View Lodge.

"He's not as bright a fugitive as everyone suspected he would be," said the D.A. "He wasn't a particularly good fugitive. They never are."

There was still no accounting for his movements during the time he was fleeing from justice, and still no trace of the murder weapon. Burke told reporters that the absence of a weapon would not affect a murder case against Dr. Sharpe, and that there was no evidence that he had received any assistance while he was on the run.

Describing the case as "domestic violence," Burke said Dr. Sharpe's motives for killing Karen would be thoroughly investigated.

"Occasionally there are incidents like this where a

restraining order cannot prevent a tragedy," he said. "It's not perfect."

Later that day a family friend read a prepared statement from Shannon Sharpe over the phone to reporters, calling for her father to be prosecuted to the fullest extent of the law.

"It should be clear that I have no doubt in my mind that my father's actions are unforgivable," she said.

While detectives were filing the necessary paperwork to extradite Richard Sharpe back to Essex County for arraignment, Shannon was at a friend's house in Newton, bravely consoling her traumatized brother and sister, along with child psychologist Dr. Sylvia Cohen. A few hours later Shannah Montessori headmistress Karen Beswick and her young son, along with Connie Behnke and her three children, arrived in Newton. The idea was to provide as familiar and secure an environment as possible for the traumatized Sharpe children.

Dr. Cohen remained with Mikey and Ali for the next five days, giving "emotional and physical support."

"Both children, especially Michael, verbalized a profound fear of their father," she later wrote in her notes, "as well as a fear that their father would come and shoot them."

Dr. Cohen observed that neither child had any love for their father, or displayed any surprise that he had murdered their mother.

"The fact that [their] primary reaction to the murder of their mother was fear of their father can be seen as indicative of a relationship with their father based on fear," she duly noted. "I would expect a child, who previously had a loving relationship with his or her father, to react with some amount of disbelief or confusion. The fact that the minor children exhibited no disbelief or confusion regarding their father after this tragedy could be interpreted to show that their relationship with their father was not a positive one."

Soon after arriving, Karen Beswick and Connie Behnke took all the children to play in a local park. Suddenly Mikey walked off by himself and into a wooded area. Beswick followed, and started talking to him.

"He just looked in my eyes and he started to cry," she remembered. "And I didn't say anything for a minute, but finally I said, 'Mikey, this is the most awful thing that will ever happen to you in your life. Nothing will ever compare to this. It's horrible what you've been through.'

"He just said to me, 'Karen, I heard the shots. I hate him!' I mean, what do you say to a seven-year-old?"

Lost for words, Beswick told the little boy that she couldn't make things better for him. Then Mikey asked if she could promise he'd never have to see his father again.

"I said, 'Yes I can,'" she remembered. "I thought, 'My God, what am I telling this child?' And then he goes, 'I know I'll never have to see him again after what he did.' And he was sobbing."

Mikey then told her that "this is the angriest my dad has ever made me," and she asked him what he did when he was angry.

"I break things when I'm angry," he replied.

Then they started walking and Beswick asked if he would feel better if he broke something now. Mikey nodded and picked up a large piece of mulch from the path.

"Karen," he said, "I don't even need my fingers, I can break this with one thumb, I'm so angry."

Then in tears, Mikey channeled all his rage against his father, picking up stick after stick, breaking them between his tiny fingers and hurling them to the ground.

"He put all his energy in that and really got into it," she said. "He needed some relief, some way of dealing with it on a seven-year-old level."

Feeling better, Mikey went back to the other children, who were playing basketball, and he joined in. A few minutes later, looking worried, he again approached Karen, who was sitting on the sidelines.

"Where are we going to go?" he asked. "What's going to happen?"

Karen told him that he and Ali would probably go and live with their Aunt Kathleen and Uncle Victor in Connecticut.

"Well, I don't want to go there!" he sobbed, walking off towards the trees.

On Monday morning, a handcuffed Richard Sharpe, dressed in orange prison fatigues, was led into Carroll County District Court, where he waived his legal right to an extradition hearing.

"I have no questions," muttered Sharpe, as a court official removed a handcuff so he could sign the waiver. Then Judge Pamela Albee remanded him into the custody of Wenham police, to be taken back to Massachusetts for arraignment on charges of first-degree murder and violating a restraining order. As he was led out to an unmarked police car, Sharpe showed no emotion and appeared to be mumbling to himself.

As Dr. Sharpe was in transit to Wenham, Jacob Atwood was appointed special administrator to Karen Sharpe's estate. He immediately filed a $100 million wrongful death suit against the doctor after hearing that his business partner, Dr. Maureen MacAloon, was about to go into probate court seeking a $3.5 million attachment on the couple's assets.

"On or about July 14th 2000, the defendant intentionally, recklessly and unlawfully discharged a rifle, fatally injuring the decedent, Karen Sharpe," wrote Atwood in his motion. "An emergency exists to protect and preserve the assets and claims of the estate."

After hearing the motion, Salem Superior Court Judge Peter Agnes froze $1.4 million of Dr. Sharpe's Merrill Lynch Individual Retirement Account as well as placing a $500,000 attachment on 8 Great Ledge Lane.

After the hearing, Atwood spoke to reporters outside the courtroom, giving them the first hints of the pain and agony Karen Sharpe had endured over the years.

"She had told everyone she knew that she was afraid he was going to kill her," he declared. "There was a lot of terrible abuse, psychological and otherwise."

Atwood explained that the wrongful death suit had been filed on behalf of Karen's three children and her family. He told reporters that Dr. Sharpe had initially sued for divorce, even though he was living with "a girlfriend" at the time.

Then Sharpe's brother Bob fired back, telling *The Boston Globe* that Karen had been trying to "swindle" millions of dollars from her husband.

"It's a terrible thing," said Bob Sharpe. "It went from a very affluent, happy family . . . to nothing."

He then accused his deceased sister-in-law of only wanting to divorce his brother after he had signed over much of his fortune to her. She was a "spendthrift," he said, buying clothes for herself and toys for the children.

This would be the beginning of bad blood between the Sharpe and Hatfield families, as they both took sides in the upcoming civil court proceedings for control of the estate and custody of the two young Sharpe children.

Late Monday night, Dr. Sharpe hired renowned Boston criminal attorney Joseph Balliro to defend him against murder charges. Known as "the Dean of the Massachusetts Defense Bar," the pugnacious, rotund 72-year-old lawyer was best known for defending reputed members of the Boston Mafia during a long and distinguished career that spanned five decades.

Balliro, who would work on the Sharpe case with his law partner and daughter, Juliane, and son, Joe Jr., had made history twenty years earlier when he defended Brad Prendergast, accused of stabbing his girlfriend to death, in the first trial in state history to allow a video camera in the courtroom.

Now, in one of the toughest cases of his career, he would be defending a man who had killed his wife in front of three witnesses.

The following morning Dr. Richard Sharpe, wearing a baggy pinstripe suit, made a brief appearance at his arraignment in Ipswich District Court. He was ordered to be held without bail after pleading innocent to killing his wife.

Showing little remorse, an ashen-faced Dr. Sharpe watched the proceedings from behind a Plexiglas enclosure, as Essex County Assistant Prosecutor Robert Weiner told Judge Robert Cornetta that Sharpe was a threat to the community.

"[He has] already exhibited a desire to flee," he argued.

Defense attorney Balliro didn't challenge Weiner, although he stated his intention of seeking bail at a later date.

"I do not concede for one moment that this is a strong case," he said optimistically.

As Sharpe left the court handcuffed and shackled, to be taken to the Essex House of Correction in Middleton, television cameras caught him tripping on a step and almost falling. This footage would be played time and again over the next eighteen months, leaving the viewing public with an indelible impression of Dr. Richard Sharpe.

On Wednesday morning, the case took a bizarre new twist. Refusing to move from the fetal position, Dr. Sharpe was deemed a suicide risk and moved to the Bridgewater State Mental Hospital. But even more sensational was the *Boston Herald*'s revelation that he was a transvestite. In a front-page story, carrying the banner headline "Doc's Dark Side: Wife Slay Suspect Was Drag Queen," the newspaper quoted a source close to the case describing how Sharpe "stole" his wife's birth control pills to grow female breasts.

The previous day an anonymous tip to all Boston-area media had revealed the existence of Karen's potentially explosive affidavit, which included pictures of the doctor in full drag. The divorce proceedings had been sealed in June at Karen Sharpe's request by Salem Probate Court, but now almost every Boston-area media outlet filed motions in probate court demanding it be made public.

"With the murder of Mrs. Sharpe and the arrest of Dr. Sharpe in connection with the alleged crime, what began as an arguably private marital dispute has recently developed into a matter of substantial public interest," wrote attorneys for the firm of Brown Rudnick Freed & Gesmer, the prestigious Boston law firm representing the *Boston Herald*. "The tragedy of domestic violence, here highlighted because the perpetrator was a respected and prominent member of the medical community, and the increased risk of harm faced by women who seek restraining orders against their abusers, are also newsworthy issues raised in this case.

"With respect to Ms. Sharpe, her previous right of privacy disappeared with her death. With respect to Mr.

Sharpe, he has now become a public figure."

Horrified that such highly embarrassing details of his violent and abusive behavior, as well as his life-long passion for women's clothes, be made public, Dr. Sharpe's civil attorney Karen Sweeney Shea filed a countermotion, demanding Karen's sworn affidavit stay secret.

"[It] may have a detrimental effect on the minor children," it argued, citing Sharpe's right of privacy under the Sixth Amendment, which guarantees the right to a fair trial.

As Salem Probate and Family Court Judge John P. Cronin considered the matter, the *Boston Herald* investigated Dr. Sharpe's close ties to the local trans-gendered community. Reporter David Wedge discovered that Sharpe's LaseHair business was used by many transsexuals, and it advertised its cosmetic procedures in the Waltham-based International Foundation for Gender Education's (IFGE) quarterly magazine *Transgender Tapestry*.

"He was a well-known name in the community," said IFGE member Nancy Cain.

But IFGE's general manager, Denise LeClair, tried to distance the group from Dr. Sharpe, claiming that he merely exploited members for business.

"He was selling his services to the community," said LeClair. "In the trans-gender community we have a lot of social events, and he never went to any of those."

Adding fuel to the media frenzy, Jacob Atwood confirmed that Sharpe gobbled Karen's birth control pills, owned a closet full of dresses and "doesn't have a hair on his body, except on his head."

The attorney said that Karen Sharpe had left him to protect Mikey from his "gender-bending" lifestyle.

"She was very concerned that her little boy would find out," he said.

Wading into the fray for the first time, Sharpe's new attorney Joe Balliro fired back, accusing Atwood of having a vested interest in the outcome of the trial and attempting "to poison the jury pool" with "garbage."

"It's shameful and unethical," he raged. "It behooves him to [insure] that [Sharpe] is found guilty."

In a bizarre coincidence, on Wednesday, as Dr. Richard Sharpe had his medical license suspended by the State Board of Registration in Medicine—declaring him an "immediate and serious threat"—two other prominent Boston-area doctors were also in court, accused of murder.

Renowned plastic surgeon Dr. James Kartell, 61, was presently on trial for shooting his wife's lover to death inside a hospital. After being found guilty of voluntary manslaughter, he was sentenced to five to eight years in jail.

"The profundity of my remorse is infinite," Dr. Kartell told the judge after his sentencing.

Meanwhile, Dr. Dirk K. Greneider, a member of the Harvard Medical faculty like Richard Sharpe, dramatically took the stand to deny bludgeoning and stabbing his wife of thirty-one years to death. Using the alter ego Thomas Young, Dr. Greneider, 60, who lived in Wellesley, Massachusetts, obsessively prowled the Internet every night and regularly met prostitutes for sex. But when his 58-year-old wife Mabel discovered his dark secret he killed her. A jury found him guilty of first-degree murder and he was sentenced to life without parole.

Dr. Kenneth Arndt, who supervised Sharpe during his residency at Harvard, said the three murderous doctors were a subject of much discussion in Boston medical circles.

"I don't think there's any colleague that I've seen that I haven't had the conversation, 'Can you believe this?' " he told the *Boston Herald*.

Chapter Eighteen

AN ADORING MOTHER

At 5:00 p.m., on July 19, the Wednesday after Karen's death, more than 350 mourners attended a memorial service at St. John's Episcopal Church on Hale Street in Beverly. Her funeral had been planned to take place the next morning, but, as if to add insult to injury, Wenham police could only legally release her body to her family for burial after her husband had signed off on it. When Sharpe deliberately stalled, the funeral had to be postponed several days.

"So even after her death, he still controls her," Karen's sister Kathleen would angrily observe a few months later. "And we couldn't bury her when we wanted to because we had to wait for him to sign [a release]. And we're sure that the prison guards went in with a pencil and a piece of paper and said, 'Sign this or you'll be sorry.' Because, believe me, if he could not have signed it, he wouldn't have."

Billed as a celebration of the life of Karen Sharpe, her friend Karen Beswick had agreed to deliver the eulogy at the thirty-five-minute private service, which was closed to the media. Originally when she was first asked to eulogize Karen, the headmistress had been reluctant, thinking a family member would be more suitable. But when no one else stepped forward, she agreed, writing a reflection of Karen through the eyes of her children.

Shannon, Mikey and Ali sat in the front row, surrounded by Karen's parents, her sister and two surviving brothers. Many at the service were moved to tears when a young Gordon College student and friend of Karen's named Sarah Herman sung Simon and Garfunkel's "Bridge Over Troubled Water" *a cappella*.

Then Karen Beswick walked slowly to the pulpit to deliver the emotionally charged sermon she dedicated to the memory of Karen Sharpe. She began by quoting one of her favorite sayings: "God cannot be everywhere, so he made mothers."

> I'm Karen Beswick, and I teach pre-school and kindergarten at Shannah Montessori, where both Mikey and Ali attended.
>
> A warm smile. A kind word. A welcoming embrace. And always unconditional generosity. Karen was an adoring mother who preferred to snuggle and be with her children than to ship them off to pre-school. 'It's only pre-school,' she would say. For it was Karen's heart that was her classroom. She planted in Shannon, Michael and Ali's hearts those seeds of love and virtue that will guide them through their journey through life.
>
> Karen was the mother we would like to be for our children. She often found humor in how very different her children could be. Shannon, the gentle, dignified young woman, Michael, the sensitive, mischievous one. Ali the free spirit.
>
> Shannon, who was still Karen's baby even

after she graduated from college, knew that her mother would embrace her friends without question and support her many ventures. If Shannon loved someone or something, so did Karen.

Karen's hand was always guided by a child's hand. The children at school always gravitated towards this warm woman who would get on the floor and admire their beautiful towers and join in their activities.

With Michael, Karen would spend hours snapping blocks together, only after they had fed Poky, our school turtle. Next, she and Mikey would inspect our daily snack table. If it didn't meet with their approval, or if it didn't include chocolate, Karen would head to the nearest sweet shop for goodies for all!

Karen would stay to help Ali wash dolls and read books to her little group of friends until we encouraged her to leave.

Every year our mothers are honored at a Mother's Day tea party with special unprovoked commentaries from their children. I would like to share Michael and Ali's special view of their mother.

From Michael: "My mom makes pancakes for me every morning. We go to the beach together for fun. We go on vacation together. She watches videos with me. She makes supper and breakfast for me. She does everything for me.

"My mom loves to play with me. We like to go to Bonkers, Discovery Zone and Chuck E. Cheese. My mom watches *Rugrats* and *Cousin Skeeter* with me. My mom likes to sleep with

me. She has too! I love her zillions and zillions.
She lets me do everything."

From Ali: "I think my mom is as tall as Shannon. We play together like hide-and-seek. She
plays tea party with me all day. We go to res-
taurants and we go to the beach and make sand
castles. We always snuggle together at night. I
have a mom so she can take care of us and
cuddle us in bed. I have a mom to read us books
and drive us to school. I have a mommy because
she loves me."

For those of us with children, we know that a
play date at Karen's could not be matched.
Karen always offered any visiting children a
party. Soda, candy, Lunchables, chocolate milk.
If she didn't have it, she would go out and get
it. As a matter of fact, it was only recently I
witnessed Karen's ability to accommodate any
child's wish. When she ran out of cherry Pop-
sicles her heart broke because a child felt left
out. Karen immediately packed six children in
the car and headed to the store to bring a smile
to that child's face.

Wherever Karen was, there were people. She
was a magnet for people who had a problem or
just wanted to chat. Maybe it was just her gen-
uine smile or laughter that made us feel better.
She was always there to offer encouraging
words or advice to young and old alike. We
were all lucky in our own way to have known
her. But none more than the three people who
got to call her Mom.

Karen, you were the mother we all aspire to

be. Our children, your children thank you. You
have nurtured these beautiful, wonderful children all alone. Now it will take a village to continue your work.

After the service, St. John's rector, the Reverend
Wendel W. Meyer, said the community had been "traumatized" by Karen's murder and had come together to
remember her good work and reach out to her family.
Calling her murder "meaningless and obscene," he said
everybody who had ever met her had been deeply af-
fected.

"She was a remarkable person who touched so many
lives," he said. "The community wanted to graft this
memory of her on its heart with the same compassion
and generosity that her life so vividly represented."

Karen Sharpe was finally laid to rest on Friday morning at a funeral service at Mount St. Peters Cemetery in
Derby, Connecticut. Later, relatives buried her ashes in
nearby Shelton.

Soon after Karen's death, purple ribbons started appearing all over Gloucester as a tribute to her memory.
The ribbons—like the ones for breast cancer or AIDS—
were organized by the locally based Help for Abused
Women and their Children (HAWC), the same group
that Dr. Mitchell Cohen had unsuccessfully urged Karen
to see while he was treating her. Scores of men and
women pinned the ribbons to their lapels, and they became a common sight around the town.

"It's a way for us to say, you know, this never should
have happened," said HAWC program coordinator, Nicole Richon Shoel. She added that the ribbons were designed to call attention to the growing problem of
domestic violence and abuse, of which Karen had become an unwilling example.

• • •

Within days of Richard Sharpe's arrest, his ClickMed
Web site was taken off the Internet and his business
empire started to crumble. For a while LaseHair stayed
afloat, run from Florida by Rich Fonte.

Initially the company president even visited Sharpe in
jail for business meetings.

"During my visits I was asked to keep the company
going," said Fonte. "He was going to turn it over to the
children eventually."

But when the prisoner started telephoning him constantly, giving ideas and advice on the running of the
company, Fonte told him to stop meddling.

"I told him I would be running the company and that
was it," he remembered. "He should continue with his
defense, and I'll take care of the company."

Before long, Sharpe's photograph and professional
profile had been removed from the LaseHair Internet
site, replaced by the message, "The profile of Dr. Richard J. Sharpe is being updated."

Paula Hiltz, who had gone into seclusion after the
murder, returned to Great Ledge Lane and soldiered on
working for the company. When Fonte offered Jacqui
Feeney her old job back, she accepted.

"I was going over to visit Paula and Rich Fonte when
I was going to work for them," she remembered. "I
didn't want to go over there, the smell of the house,
everything. I missed the kids. I started going out to demo
for LaseHair, but my heart wasn't in it."

During the thirty days he was at Bridgewater State
Mental Hospital, Sharpe was kept under close observa-
tional status, in case he attempted suicide. In their daily
sessions, his attending psychiatrist, Dr. Gilbert Bogen,
had the opportunity to observe him closely. He noticed

that Sharpe would behave normally—watching television, talking to the other inmates or lying across three chairs to relax—when he thought no one was watching. But if a doctor walked in, Sharpe underwent a dramatic change.

"When we were face-to-face he would close his eyes, squint, as if he was in pain," remembered Dr. Bogen. "This was something I did not see at a distance. When he was on the phone or watching TV, he was quite relaxed and had no indication of distress or pain. In my opinion, he was malingering."

On Tuesday, July 25, Probate Court Judge John Cronin ordered the Sharpe divorce papers to be unsealed, finding that most of the juicy bits had already been leaked to the press by Jacob Atwood.

"Much of the information which the parties sought to protect from public disclosure and from disclosure to their children, has now been widely disclosed in the press," wrote the judge in his ruling. "Some of the information has apparently been supplied to the press by counsel representing the interests of some family members.

Outside the courtroom a triumphant Atwood told reporters, "We don't want Karen's voice to be silenced."

Three months later, Sharpe would write down his thoughts about the case, which was fast gaining international attention, appearing in newspapers as far away as England and Australia. Amazingly, he blamed Jacob Atwood and the media for causing distress to his children.

"As each day goes by, it seems that the media, with direction by that malevolent liar, Jacob Atwood, paints me even blacker," Inmate #3445 wrote from his jail cell. "I don't know how Karen found Atwood, but my family doesn't deserve him. Shannon is being used by him as a pawn to enhance his '15-minutes-of-fame.' I worry that Mikey and Ali will be further hurt by the outrageous publicity.

"I try my best to minimize publicity (avoiding court appearances, etc.) but it just keeps on coming, and is even more malignant with each iteration.

"I'm not sure what the best course is to protect Mike and Ali from this. I do however believe that anything that enhances publicity harms Mike and Ali."

Immediately after Judge Cronin's ruling, Richard Sharpe's lawyers appealed to the state's highest court, and the divorce papers were ordered to remain sealed until a state appeals judge had time to review the opposing motions.

Chapter Nineteen

SUFFER THE LITTLE CHILDREN

On Monday, July 24, 2000, Shannon Sharpe and her aunt and uncle, Kathleen and Victor Lembo, officially asked the probate and family court for temporary custody of Mikey and Ali. In three separate emergency motions, filed without notifying Richard Sharpe, they expressed "fear" that he would try and block them as guardians out of spite.

"The petitioners are exceedingly concerned for the well being of the minor children in the light of the cold-blooded murder of their mother," read Shannon's motion, "further exacerbated by the excessive media attention surrounding this tragedy."

Kathleen Lembo noted that the resulting publicity from their mother's murder, has caused "anguish and embarrassment" for both children, who are in need of "care, compassion and stability," in a "warm, stable environment."

"My husband Victor and I have two daughters of our own and we reside in a Connecticut suburb, Beacon Falls," she wrote. "Victor is ordained as a Christian minister and we are both active within our community. Our extended family, including Michael and Alexandra's grandparents and uncles, live in close proximity to us in Connecticut."

The court agreed, immediately appointing them temporary guardians of Mikey and Ali, until a more permanent ruling could be made.

On Tuesday, August 1, an Essex County Grand Jury indicted Richard Sharpe for the first-degree murder of his wife, illegal weapon possession and violating a restraining order. He was ordered to be arraigned at Salem Superior Court on August 10. His attorney Joe Balliro said his client would plead not guilty to all charges, but he had still not decided whether to ask for bail at the arraignment.

Desperately short of money, and not being able to afford Balliro's retainer, Sharpe sold off LaseHair's three lasers, two Dermabrasion machines and an IBM ThinkPad laptop computer for $70,000 to his brother Robert's Pine Corporation of Shelton, Connecticut. He also transferred ownership of the rest of his medical and dermatological equipment to Joe Balliro, as well as nearly $40,000.

After hearing that his daughter Shannon and the Lembos had been given custody of Mikey and Ali, a furious Richard Sharpe lashed out from the Bridgewater State Mental Hospital, where he was still being treated. First he evicted Shannon from her apartment adjoining the house in Great Ledge Lane and attempted to prevent her from removing her possessions. She had to get a court order, over Joe Balliro's strenuous objections, to retrieve her belongings. A police escort was present when she arrived to take her furniture, a piano, and Mikey and Ali's toys and pet reptiles. After the house was cleared it was then turned over to Sharpe's brother Robert.

"This has been very difficult for Shannon," said Atwood's law partner, Mark Smith, who went to Lawrence Housing Court on her behalf. "She has moments when she just breaks down."

Two days later, on August 4, Richard Sharpe filed a family court motion, opposing Shannon being appointed temporary guardian of Mikey and Ali. In a furious and often rambling eleven-point motion, handwritten by Joe Balliro's daughter and law partner Juliane, it raged at Shannon for daring to criticize Sharpe after he'd killed her mother.

"Shannon Sharpe has openly and publicly declared her intention to do everything in her power to destroy [me]," it began. "She has been openly contemptuous of [me] without regard to the negative impact of her contempt on the emotional well-being of the minor children. Shannon has openly and publicly declared her contempt for [me]."

He also stated his intention to fight for access to his children in prison, voicing his concern that Shannon would "disparage" him to the children and try to turn them against him.

The next day Probate Court Judge Cronin rejected Sharpe's objections out of hand, ruling that Shannon and her aunt and uncle would continue guardianship of Mikey and Ali. Then, taking aim at Sharpe, he said that living in a wholesome family setting would help them "salvage some of their fragile emotions from childhood."

On Thursday, August 10, Shannon Sharpe saw her father for the first time since her mother's murder, when he was arraigned at Salem Superior Court.

The proceedings were delayed two hours after guards forgot to bring Sharpe's suit from Middleton Jail. Finally he appeared in the dock, wearing the same baggy pin-stripe suit, white shirt and tie he had worn at his previous arraignment. Sharpe attempted to make eye contact with

Shannon, but she refused to even acknowledge him.

Then, after feebly pleading not guilty to first-degree murder and the two lesser charges, he was returned to Bridgewater State Mental Hospital for at least thirty more days, to be evaluated for mental illness. As he was led out of the courtroom he tried to talk to his daughter. Shannon's piercing eyes looked straight ahead. She completely ignored him.

One month to the day after Karen Sharpe died, one hundred and fifty of her friends and other well-wishers, all wearing purple ribbons, gathered at Walker Creek Bridge, behind Great Ledge Lane, for a candlelight memorial in her honor. A light evening rain fell as they solemnly walked across the little white bridge to a secluded marsh at Walker Street, which had been one of Karen's favorite places to play with Mikey and Ali.

After a moment of silence, they all recited a passage together, vowing, "As long as we live, she will too, for she is a part of us."

The evening, organized by a group of Karen's friends, was also a fund-raiser for HAWC to help other abused women in Gloucester. They raised $2,200 for HAWC, including $450 from the Shannah Montessori parents and children.

Nicole Richon Shoel spoke at the vigil, saying that, although she had never met Karen Sharpe, she had learned that she was a "kind person in an often unkind world."

Then sadly addressing the many years of abuse Karen had suffered at the hands of her husband, she described her as the victim of a "hushed and private violence."

Karen's friend and neighbor Carol Figurido, who had been on the cruise the night she died, told the gathering that she could feel Karen's presence.

"I can just see her now with her legs crossed, just smiling at us all," Figurido confided. "She enjoyed every precious moment with her children. I often said she had the patience of a saint. She would just laugh and shrug it off."

Then, after assuring them that their friend was now in a better place, she urged everyone never to forget Karen, declaring: "Tonight we are joined so that your voice will never be silenced."

On August 29, Kristen Dormitzer filed a five-million-dollar suit against Sharpe. The nineteen-year-old baby-sitter claimed that witnessing Karen Sharpe's murder had caused her emotional stress, recurring nightmares, nausea and headaches.

"There can be little doubt that the heinous crime was a significantly traumatic incident that will haunt her for the rest of her life," read her motion, filed by her attorney, John Weltman.

Calling Dormitzer a hero, Weltman said he was particularly struck by her first instinct of running to save the kids from imminent danger.

"She is genuinely injured, genuinely in pain and I wanted to help her," he told reporters.

Middlesex Superior Court Judge Raymond Brassard also approved an $850,000 attachment against Sharpe's assets, to stop them being liquidated before her case could come to court.

A year later Dormitzer would describe her vivid impressions of that terrible night.

"I can still hear the echoes and loud sounds of hearts beating and stopping," she wrote. "The term blood, sweat and tears reveals a new meaning to me. All these pictures keep appearing in my head of Karen—seeing her try to run, and Mikey's face when I got to him.

"I remember thinking, 'God, please get us out. Tell me she's not dead.'

"I think about earlier in the day. What was I like? Did I know that my life would change forever? Did Karen know hers would end? What was I like at 11:45 p.m. before I felt the heat from the bullet that killed Karen?"

As Richard Sharpe languished in Bridgewater State Mental Hospital, he watched the remains of his fortune disappear. In mid-August, Shannon and the Lembos went to court to freeze his assets, including his stock portfolio and bank accounts, as well as demanding he pay child support for Mikey and Ali. A probate and family court judge agreed, ordering Sharpe not to dispose of anything or attempt to change his will. He was also ordered to pay $1,130.00 a week towards the support of his children.

The last nail in the coffin of his business empire came on August 14, when seven of Karen's neighbors from Great Ledge Lane petitioned the Gloucester Police Department to close down LaseHair, which was operating illegally in a residential zone. Three days later building inspector John Barrigan, accompanied by two police detectives, searched the house, confirming that it was being used as a business. A month later, the city of Gloucester ordered Sharpe to move LaseHair out of the house immediately. Within a few weeks LaseHair was history, as its eighteen affiliates reopened their hair-removal businesses under different names, wanting nothing more to do with Sharpe.

"We helped empty out the offices," said former LaseHair employee Jacqui Feeney. "And it was kind of a closure for me."

Chapter Twenty

IN HIS OWN WRITE

While the Supreme Judicial Court of Massachusetts pondered whether to unseal the potentially explosive Sharpe divorce papers, Shannon Sharpe preempted them. Furious at her father's request for a court-ordered psychiatrist to examine Mikey and Ali, in an attempt to gain future visitations and regular telephone contact with them, Shannon filed her own opposing motion into the public domain. It contained horrific new incidents of abuse, as well as releasing three damning photos of her father in full drag, to discredit Joe Balliro's claims that his client was not a cross-dresser.

Quoting Shakespeare, Jacob Atwood, who filed the affidavits on behalf of the family, said Sharpe's stated intention to resume a parental role in his children's lives only shows that he is "brushed by the wings of madness."

On October 17, 2000, the *Boston Herald* carried the pictures of Sharpe in women's clothes on its front page, along with Shannon's new revelations that he had once thrown acid in her mother's face and had tried to poison them both.

In her affidavit, Shannon said she had released the pictures, showing her father posing seductively in slinky dresses and a wig, to prove he was unfit to have any contact with her young brother and sister.

"I implore the Court to deny such a request," she wrote, "which I sincerely believe would irreparably harm both of my siblings."

In her six-page sworn affidavit, Shannon described in detail how her father had terrorized the family for years, using violence and blackmail to control them.

"I have attached as Exhibit 'A' various pictures of Richard dressed as a woman, which were taken over the course of the past several years," she wrote. "My mother retained these pictures to undercut Richard's threatened attempts to obtain custody of Michael and Alexandra, which he always threatened. Richard's attorney, Joseph Balliro, has suggested to the media that the allegation that Richard is a cross-dresser is 'bogus.' To the contrary, Richard *is* a cross-dresser."

She then went on to reveal how her father would "habitually" take her and her mother's underwear from their bureaus, swallowed Karen's birth control pills to grow breasts, and had recently become increasingly more active in the "transgender community."

"One of the primary reasons why my mother left Richard was to shield Michael from exposure to Richard's practices at his impressionable age," she wrote.

Saying that her little brother and sister had "endured a lifetime of grief," she said she and their aunt and uncle were trying to give Mikey and Ali the "stability, love and a sense of security" that were "stolen" when Richard killed their mother.

"Now the man who robbed them of their childhood, and left them orphans, requests this Court to order the children to resume contact with them. I remain hopeful that the Court recognizes the trauma which the children have endured and will protect the children's best interests by denying Richard Sharpe's requests."

Shannon's damning affidavit was accompanied by similar ones from Jamie Hatfield, Christine Regan, Karen Beswick, Dr. Sylvia Cohen and child psychologist Dr. Kelly Tahaney–Weber, who had been counseling Mikey and Ali since their mother's killing.

"The children are beginning to cope with their difficult loss," Tahaney–Weber wrote. "This favorable adjustment is due, in large part, to the stability that the Lembo home is providing for the children, coupled with the proactive efforts of their aunt, uncle and sister to support the children through this crisis and shelter them from potential threats to their stability.

During her regular family counseling sessions, Dr. Tahaney–Weber found Mikey and Ali to have "experienced difficulty processing the events surrounding their mother's death," as well as "anxiousness and avoidance" when the subject was raised.

"They also exhibited anxiety and avoidance regarding their relationship with their father," she claimed. "The processing of this loss and other traumatic events they have witnessed will be a slow process and will progress at the children's pace."

Citing their father as the main threat to his children, Dr. Tahaney–Weber urged the court to deny his request to resume contact with them.

"As the alleged perpetrator of their mother's murder and alleged perpetrator of domestic violence, which the children were reported to have witnessed, Richard Sharpe's request warrants very careful scrutiny."

Joseph Balliro immediately attacked Shannon, calling her new allegations "fabrications," and the photos of his client in drag merely advertisements for LaseHair.

"His wife even helped him get dressed," he told the *Boston Herald*, admitting that he had not yet seen the photographs.

The following day, at a hearing to determine if Sharpe, who was not present, should be allowed visitations with Mikey and Ali, Essex Probate and Family Court Judge John C. Stevens III denied his request. But he did appoint a psychiatrist from Massachusetts General Hospital to interview the children, members of the family and anyone relevant to the case, and make recommendations as to whether Sharpe should be allowed parental contact, and to report back within ninety days.

Soon after the pictures of him in drag were splashed across the front pages of newspapers across America, Richard Sharpe attempted suicide. While being examined by a nurse, with a correctional officer in attendance, in the infirmary at Middleton Jail, having been returned from Bridgewater State Mental Hospital, Sharpe brazenly got up from his chair and helped himself to a vial of mumps vaccine, thinking it was insulin.

"The nurse and the officer were stunned," said a spokesman for the jail. "They saw him do it."

The spokesman said that Sharpe was never in any real danger, as he only grabbed a single dose. He had been punished with ten days in disciplinary lockup. Amazingly, while in solitary, Sharpe entered into secret negotiations to write a book about the case. Former journalist Dr. Cynthia Bjorlie, his landlord at Cape Ann Medical Center in the mid-90s, read about the case and wrote him a letter.

"I had this idea that I should write about Richard and his personality," said the doctor, a published freelance author, who once wrote trailers for TV shows. "He accepted it."

On October 25, Sharpe sat down in his cell and wrote Dr. Bjorlie a six-page letter, giving her an overview of his life with Karen and her murder, from his own jaundiced perspective.

"I myself don't understand this nightmare," he began.

Then he described a "typical" day in the Sharpe family household, making it sound like an episode straight out of *Ozzie and Harriet.*

"It would start with Karen and I waking up in our large waterbed," he wrote Dr. Bjorlie. "Ninety percent of the time Michael, Ali or both kids either slept with us, or made their way into the bedroom at night." He later went on to tell how Ali occasionally wet the bed, calling it a "small price to pay" for the family's happiness.

Sharpe told Bjorlie how their pet dogs Fluffy, a Lhasa apso, and Cocoa, a golden retriever, slept on the stoop at Great Ledge Lane, to guard the family.

"Nights in our Gloucester house were warm," he wrote. "Emotionally secure and something to long for, even on terrible days."

When the family woke up, according to Sharpe, he would watch children's TV programs with Mikey and Ali, or they would play with the dogs before he drove them to school. After he returned from working out in the gym, he spent quality time with the kids, reading them stories or playing in the bath together, with wind-up submarines and stuffed animals.

"Michael liked to tease me," he wrote, "by splashing me or even squirting me with a squirt gun."

But according to Sharpe, everything changed in December 1999 when Karen first saw 19 Hull Street.

"Karen pushed to buy the Wenham house and won," he maintained. "Our plan was to buy [it], finish most of the work by May, so we could then move in and sell the Gloucester house."

Then on the advice of an estate planning lawyer, Sharpe told how he transferred $2.9 million and the new house into Karen's name, saying that he had completely trusted her. He then described how Karen had walked out on him in February, without a word of explanation.

"Over the following weeks and months a scenario unfolded, which included Karen having an affair with Marc Beauregard, the painter who she hired as a contractor on the new house, embezzlement of money from the laser hair removal business by Karen, with transfers to Marc."

He then addressed the recent newspaper revelations of the "cross-dressing nonsense," claiming he had only done it as an "impulse thing," while selling cosmetic procedures at a trans-gender conference the previous January.

"Jacob Atwood has taken this harmless prank and twisted it into a media circus," he complained.

Then he self-piteously wrote that, now that Karen was "gone," the only thing he could hold onto was the "possibility that Ali and Michael may need me."

Writing that he had probably revealed more than his attorney would have liked, Sharpe seemed delighted that his recent suicide attempt had made the news.

"I grabbed a vial, hoping it was insulin," he wrote, "but it was a skin test antigen. Sorry about the candid thoughts."

He then invited Dr. Bjorlie to visit him in jail, saying his telephone calls were monitored and his incoming mail was opened.

"Call ahead for the visit schedule and also ask if I can have visitors," said Sharpe. "I have been locked up for everything from looking at someone the wrong way, to I guess the valid reason of trying to grab a drug to do myself in."

A few days later Dr. Bjorlie visited him in Middleton Jail and she questioned him about Karen and why he killed her.

"[He said] he loved her," Dr. Bjorlie would later testify. "That he wished none of this had happened."

Even though the other 120 inmates at Middleton Jail knew he was a transvestite, having seen the embarrassing pictures on television news, Richard Sharpe encountered little hostility behind bars. Before long he had even made friends in the jail, helping fellow prisoners write letters home and giving them medical advice.

"It is kind of interesting," said Sheriff Frank Cousins Jr., who runs the jail. "The other inmates do take a liking to him and a lot of people are surprised by that."

Sheriff Cousins said Sharpe liked to chat and mingle with fellow prisoners, only seeming distressed when he had been put in solitary after stealing the mumps vaccine.

On Thursday, November 2, Jacob Atwood and his law associate, Erin Shapiro, arrived at the Middleton Correctional Center at 11:00 a.m. to apprise Sharpe of his current financial situation, as it related to the $100 million wrongful death suit brought by Karen's estate. Dressed in Day-Glo orange prison garb, Sharpe bristled with anger as he was led into a conference room for the face-to-face confrontation with Atwood, originally scheduled to take place in July, three days after Karen's murder. Also present were Joe Balliro and his daughter Juliane.

Immediately after Sharpe was sworn in, Atwood went on the offensive.

"I believe it's Mr. Sharpe?" he asked. "Would you please identify yourself?

"*Doctor* Richard Sharpe," answered the prisoner, defiantly.

"Are you a medical doctor?" asked Atwood.

"Yes."

"Has not your license been taken away?"

"Just a minute," said Balliro, as he went to confer with his client.

"I'm invoking my Fifth Amendment," muttered Sharpe, after consulting his lawyer.

From then on Sharpe took the Fifth to all Atwood's subsequent questions, until Balliro stepped in asking the deposition be brought to an end.

"I think that any further questioning of Dr. Sharpe is going to be extremely detrimental to his health," reasoned Balliro. "To continue this deposition is going to be unnecessarily cruel, harassing and harmful to Dr. Sharpe. This deposition is over as far as I'm concerned, Mr. Atwood."

Balliro then ordered Middleton warden Captain Richard Nangle to return Sharpe to his cell, effectively ending the proceedings.

Two weeks later Joe Balliro announced that at his trial, now scheduled for next July, Richard Sharpe would plead insanity. One of *the* most difficult defenses in the Massachusetts legal system, Balliro had an uphill battle on his hands. He would have to prove beyond reasonable doubt that his client was unable to conform his conduct to the requirements of the law, and lacked the capacity to appreciate the criminality or wrongfulness when he shot his wife to death.

"That is the only reasonable way he can defend himself," Essex County Assistant D.A. Bob Weiner told the *Boston Herald*. "He shot his wife in front of people that knew him."

A few days after Cynthia Bjorlie visited him in jail,
Sharpe wrote her a second letter, filling in background
for the "project" they were now collaborating on. Saying
he didn't know how much longer he could be "patient,"
as Balliro had asked him to be, he wrote of how he had
first met Karen in spring 1972 at Shelton High School,
and their subsequent courtship and marriage.

"I loved Karen very much," he said, "and I miss her."

In his sanitized version there was no mention of the
violence and abuse that marred their marriage, and he
even claimed it had been *him* who had wanted a divorce
in 1991.

"Karen talked me into giving our relationship another
chance," he wrote, carefully omitting how he had repeatedly stabbed her with a fork leading to his involuntary committal to a mental institution.

He wrote at length about Ali's birth and how he had
saved his daughter's life after her condition had been
misdiagnosed at the hospital. Then he finished the letter
with a rambling denouncement of Jacob Atwood, accusing him of "malevolence" and trying to blacken his good
name.

That Thanksgiving, wallowing in self-pity, Sharpe
wrote Dr. Bjorlie that he had fallen into a deep depression and was contemplating suicide. Once again showing
no remorse whatsoever, he appeared to blame Karen for
his predicament.

"Thanksgiving should be a time of giving thanks for
health, family, friends and a reasonable level of material
worth," wrote the man who had always shunned the holiday season. "However, there is a distinction between
wealth and greed."

Appearing to cast Karen as the greedy partner in the marriage, he said *she* had fallen in love with the "decadent" Wenham house. Then he said he had been "devastated" by her refusal to allow him to see where his children would grow up.

On one occasion, soon after his March accident, he wrote of driving by the house and seeing Mikey and Ali playing by the pond.

"I parked in the driveway and on crutches set out towards Mike and Ali. Mike came running to greet me. Karen saw me, and initially demanded that I leave. After a brief 'discussion,' she said that she would allow me to visit the kids for a while at the pond.

"The emotional pain was far greater than the physical pain. I stayed for about one-and-a-half hours, at which time I was exhausted due to my recent physical injuries.

"When I went home, I went to bed and the sense of isolation, abandonment, betrayal and depression was profound. It took a combination of two Percocets and a Klonopin to induce a brief withdrawal into the safety and calm of sleep."

Several days later, wrote Sharpe, Karen broke a verbal agreement to bring the kids to Great Ledge Lane, refusing to pick up the telephone when he called. He then drove to Hull Street, where he saw his children playing in the front yard. He broke down in tears as he watched them.

"After regaining my composure I pulled into the driveway," he wrote. "Mike and Ali ran towards the car. Karen saw them and started yelling alternately at them and me, scaring the children. I left and cried most of the day in the big, cold, yet once warm Gloucester house. The house was as empty as I was."

Complaining that prison doctors now had him on a debilitating "cocktail of anti-depressants," he said he doubted he could survive without contact with his children.

"When Karen left, unexpectedly in February with 3 million dollars, title to the Wenham home and Mike and Ali, I wonder if she realized that the only 'wealth' was the children? Karen and I should have been celebrating our 'wealth' today as a complete family."

Chapter Twenty-one

JAILBREAK

As Christmas approached, Richard Sharpe decided to escape from Essex House of Correction. He recruited a fellow inmate named Steven L. Smith, offering him 1 million dollars to get "some boys" on the outside, who would be prepared to kill police. Boasting that he was a multi-millionaire, he gave Smith information about his Merrill Lynch IRA account, which he verified had $835,000 in it.

Smith then agreed to accept an advance of $25,000 to $50,000, with the rest coming after he'd gone abroad.

"And of course, I think, 'Grab the up-front money and run,'" Smith would later admit. "Dr. Sharpe wanted me to get boys that would kill police if necessary. I thought him deranged."

A self-confessed con-man, Smith then agreed to Sharpe's request to have a friend set up a three-way calling system, so he could make phone calls from jail without the authorities being able to monitor them. Sharpe assured him his advance would more than cover the cost of the calls.

And to raise even more money for the escape, according to Smith, Sharpe planned to ask Smith's mother to file a bogus claim against his own medical insurance company, personally writing two letters claiming that two of his nurses had performed liposuction, resulting in nerve damage.

Smith also claimed that Sharpe gave him personal information about Karen, telling him, "Use this to open a credit card account and raise money for my escape."

Over the next few months—as they plotted the escape—Sharpe ran up a $500 phone bill, repeatedly calling Shannon and the Lembos, attempting to contact Mikey and Ali. He also telephoned his friend and former employee Jacqui Feeney so often in the weeks leading up to Christmas that her boyfriend Scott Kilman put a block on the phone to prevent his calls.

"Sharpe was calling from Middleton all the time," said Kilman, who had already been interviewed several times by the D.A.'s office about Sharpe's break-in into Karen's motel room. "My attorney told me to get as far away from him as possible."

But Feeney still felt drawn to her old boss, fondly remembering the good times they'd had at LaseHair, and started visiting him twice a week at Middleton Jail.

"I didn't really want to at first," she admitted. "And then at Christmas-time I felt sorry for him, and went to see him. I had always felt comfortable with him and it was good to see him in jail. It was like he was normal and nothing had happened."

During her visits, Sharpe played the sympathy card, telling Feeney she was the only one standing by him in his time of need, and her visits were the only thing that "kept him hanging on."

Feeney found the jailhouse visits emotionally draining, as Sharpe endlessly bewailed his plight, saying how much he missed his family. But he still boasted of getting high in jail, saying friends were smuggling him Percodan, disguised as vitamin C tablets.

Then, during one visit, she asked him about Karen's murder.

"He did that eye-rubbing thing," she recounted. "He claims he doesn't remember. He says he threw the gun out. He tossed it, but he didn't know where."

In January 2001, his old friend and former University of Bridgeport classmate, Dawn Ward, who years earlier had moved away to Pennsylvania and lost touch, wrote to him at Middleton after hearing about Karen's murder. Sharpe replied immediately and soon Ward and her daughter Sophia Duly, who used to babysit Shannon, were both regular visitors and in daily communication with him.

"My mother called me to tell me what had happened," said Duly. "I sat down and wrote a simple note to him, saying my thoughts and prayers are with him during this time of crisis."

For the next few months he cultivated a friendship with Dawn and Sophia, having them run errands and generally do his bidding. They became his two staunchest supporters, facilitating Sharpe's three-way phone calls and willingly picking up the tab out of friendship.

His brother Ben also visited him several times over this period. When Ben asked him if he had murdered Karen, Sharpe was evasive, replying: "What do you think?"

And when his sister Laurie, who never once visited him in jail, but often spoke with him on the phone, broached the subject of Karen's death, Sharpe said he couldn't discuss "these things" on the phone.

He even received a marriage proposal from a middle-aged woman who'd started visiting him in jail. Although she claimed to be a psychiatrist, a subsequent police investigation revealed that she was a crank, and she was banned from visiting him.

In January 2002, *Boston Magazine* ran a twelve-page cover story on the Sharpe case, entitled: "Femme Fatale." Reporter Gretchen Voss had secured Shannon's cooperation for the in-depth article, complete with a full-page color picture of Sharpe in a slinky, low-cut blouse, black wig and fishnet stockings, with the caption, "Sharpe Dressed Man."

The feature provided a frightening blow-by-blow account of the abuse Karen and Shannon had suffered from Dr. Sharpe, causing a sensation in Boston. Three weeks later, Dr. Cynthia Bjorlie told Sharpe she wanted to write a book on his case, and had a publisher in mind. The inmate said he needed time to consider the idea and run it past Joe Balliro, asking how much money it would generate towards his growing legal bills.

On January 20, he wrote Dr. Bjorlie, saying he was at an all-time low, and had just met Father Curren, the Catholic prison priest, asking him to call his brother-in-law Victor Lembo to tell his children he missed them.

"Last year at this time my only significant worry was the Y-2K compliance of my medical software," he wrote. "My deeply emotional crying spells have been in check for two days. Even though all days are alike, I am more depressed on weekends and holidays. I suspect this is because these were times when my non-stop work schedule would lapse a bit and I would have more time with my family."

He also told her he had met "some good people" in jail, although many of the inmates were people he would never want to know on the outside.

"Living in jail is 'no life,' as my friend Sandy Laba says. Sandy is getting out in four weeks, and when I seem depressed, tries to cheer me up with a mix of broken English and Spanish ('Labish,' as I call it). Just today he said he had a dream we were in the tropics, playing with children."

After Father Curren failed to get any response from Victor Lembo, Sharpe stepped up his campaign to reunite with his children. He started leaving messages on Shannon's answering machine at the Lembos' house in Connecticut, and writing her letters, begging her to visit him at Middleton. After receiving each letter, she would immediately fax them over to Jacob Atwood's office and the Essex County Prosecutor's Office, giving them further ammunition against her father.

On January 22, he wrote:

> Dear Shannon:
>   Please come and visit so that we can talk. I love you, talking can only help both of us.
>   I believe that anything we do should only be in the best interest of Ali & Mike.
>   I miss you and will always love you unconditionally,
>
> Sincerely,
Dad
>
>   P.S. "Visits" are every 4 days. I am on 240A. Call ahead for the visit schedule.

Two weeks later, after receiving no word from Shannon, he wrote again, marking the envelope "confidential":

Dear Shannon:

    I love you, Mike & Ali.

    Please visit me.

Love Dad

    P.S. Why don't you take over the laser business?

Once again Shannon ignored him, not wanting anything to do with her father. And on Valentine's Day he sent a third letter, saying he had loved her mother and pleading for another chance to be a father to his children.

Dear Shannon:

    I loved your mother. I miss her terribly. I cry everyday. I want nothing but the best for you, Mike & Ali. The only thing that gets me through each day is the thought that my children may need me.

    I wish you would find the courage to visit me and talk to me face-to-face.

    Shannon, I love you! I love Mike & Ali. I didn't spend enough time with you when you were growing up. Both Karen and I did the impossible. With very little outside help, we both went to school and went into successful careers. We both should be kicking back and enjoying the fruits of our hard work. Now, instead everything is gone. I have always worried that my children would be forced to work through hardships like Karen and I, so I had to insure against this. I set up trusts for Mike & Ali. I was in the process of setting up a trust for you when Karen left.

My life is over. I would gladly trade places with Karen.

Shannon, this letter is private, please do not show it to anyone, especially that evil bastard Atwood.

Come and talk to me.

Love Dad.

Over the next six weeks, he called Shannon repeatedly but she would never answer her phone. Finally, in late March, he wrote one last time.

Dear Shannon:

I've tried to call you a number of times, but all I get is voicemail. I really want to talk to you. I would prefer it if you would visit me, and that is really the only way we can have a confidential conversation. Ben would also like to talk to you. Ben's intentions have been and always will be good. When I last spoke to Ben, yesterday, he said that the "estate lawyer" called him and that she said that you sent me a letter. I don't know if that was a misunderstanding, but if it wasn't and you did send a letter, I didn't receive it.

Shannon, I will always have unconditional love for you, Mike & Ali. I loved your mother with all my heart. I miss Karen and would do anything to have this nightmare go away and have our family back.

Please contact me.

Love Dad

On April 23, Essex County Assistant D.A. Richard Weiner asked Suffolk Superior Court Judge Christine

McEvoy, who would try the case, to prevent Inmate Sharpe from "harassing" his daughter Shannon. The judge said there was no law to stop him from communicating with his children, but warned that anything he said or wrote could be used in evidence against him at his upcoming trial.

Two weeks earlier, on Saturday, April 7, a court-ordered psychiatrist, Dr. Malcolm Rogers, went to Middleton Jail to examine Richard Sharpe for the prosecution. Ironically Dr. Rogers was an Associate Clinical Professor of Psychiatry at Harvard Medical School, and a member of the faculty, as Sharpe had once been.

Dr. Rogers, who had already interviewed most of the key players in the case, had arranged for a video crew to film the interview, which was conducted in an office at the jail. When he was brought into the room by a guard, Sharpe appeared "anxious," saying he didn't think he could do the three-hour interview in front of a camera and the lights.

"He complained of being dizzy," said Dr. Rogers. "The lights were turned down and we got him some food and water."

Then the interview started and at one point Dr. Rogers called a break, leaving Sharpe alone in the office.

"There was a monitor outside the room," Dr. Rogers would later testify. "When I was out of the room, I observed on the monitor the defendant going through my notes."

When the psychiatrist returned to continue the interview he never mentioned the incident, but later in the discussion he deliberately went out again, and watched Sharpe on the monitor sneaking another look at his notes.

•   •   •

In spring 2001, Sharpe and inmate Steven Smith drafted several plans for his jail escape on paper. Sharpe had initially suggested that Smith fake a urinary problem, so he would receive a drug called Hytrin. According to his plan, Sharpe would then deliberately overdose on the drug and be taken to the emergency room at Beverly Hospital, where Smith's "boys" would overpower the guards and free him. But the plan was aborted after Smith feigned a urinary problem, receiving several painful examinations but no drugs.

Then in early May, Sharpe was ordered to undergo a CAT scan at Massachusetts General Hospital, and he formulated a back-up plan. Well acquainted with the layout of the hospital from his days as a doctor, Sharpe wrote out a plan for Steven Smith's outside accomplices to follow. It read like a bad gangster movie, complete with code-words and written in the third person, in case it was intercepted by guards.

SUMMARY

On May 14th, the subject has an appointment at the MGH [Massachusetts General Hospital] at 10 a.m. He will almost certainly be dropped off at the main entrance between 8:15 and 10:15 a.m. by Essex County or Suffolk County Sherrif [sic] Deputies. The two deputies will have guns, the inmate will be shackled. The inmate will be escorted to the Bigelow Building and will be taken to the 12th floor for an EEG test. This test will take roughly an hour. The subject will then either be taken to the Founder's Building, First Floor, for an MRI test or be taken to the Nashua Street Jail and then back for the MRI. The MRI will be done between 12 and 4:00 p.m. The subject will then be taken

*back to Middleton. The best bet for snatching
the subject is between 8:15 a.m. and 10:15 a.m.
when he is dropped at the MGH entrance.*

*Do not reference this directly on the phone. If
it is a go, say "Grandma will visit in May." If
it is not a go, say "Grandma will not visit in
May."*

*Everyone will be well compensated. After the
subject is snatched, he will be brought to Connecticut and will travel out of the country only
when a second payment is recieved [sic].*

*The subject will preferably be driven out of the
country and a bonus payment will be paid after
he arrives in another country.*

*The "insurance" will provide an additional in-
centive for you!*

Unfortunately for Sharpe, Steven Smith happened to
read a story in the *Boston Herald*, reporting how Essex
County Probate Court had frozen his Merrill Lynch IRA
fund. He realized that Sharpe had scammed him, and
had no available funds.

"I confronted him," Smith later claimed, "and he said,
'So what, the transfer form will still go through. I'm
facing murder. Big deal.' That's when I wanted to punch
him in the face."

After being transferred to a prison in Connecticut,
Smith wrote a letter to Essex County D.A. Kevin Burke,
revealing Sharpe's escape plan. He later tried to sell the
story to the *Boston Herald*.

"Nothing this guy did was legit," complained Smith,
adding that he had no qualms to "rat" him out.

• • •

Richard Sharpe's projected book with Dr. Cynthia Bjorlie was put on hold when Joe Balliro found out about it, and ordered him to stop writing anything down that could later be used against him.

"If I had known this was the case up-front," wrote Dr. Sharpe referring to the "Project," "I certainly would not have been so open and soul-searching."

Nevertheless he continued writing to Dr. Bjorlie, complaining about the "bland, mechanical routine" of prison life, blaming Jacob Atwood for "fanning the media flames." He also questioned whether Shannon was "laughing and smirking" at him in "some kind of self-centered, vindictive game."

"My maternal grandfather was deeply religious," he wrote in one of his last letters to Bjorlie, referring to the relative who had hanged himself. "When I am in such a deep depression that I can't concentrate, I read the Bible."

Reminding her again to keep all his "written and oral communications confidential," Sharpe claimed to have been sexually humiliated by prison guards, during a routine strip-search after a court appearance.

"The guard had me bend over to inspect my anus," he wrote. "He then said, 'I think you 'tucked something!' He summoned two other guards and they inspected me with a flashlight, making jokes the whole time. I worry about the more violent inmates and have been lucky several times when I was threatened and had a couple of tougher inmates intervene to help me."

After telling Dr. Bjorlie to put her book on hold until after the "tragedy recedes," Sharpe invited Dawn Ward's daughter, Sophia Duly, who had a journalism degree, to be his new literary collaborator.

"Richie wants me to write a book," said Duly. "I'll be blunt with you, he needs money."

Duly, who was seeking a co-writer for the book, claimed access to a thousand-page diary that Sharpe had been writing since his incarceration, as well as never-before-seen photographs.

"I've got a gold mine of information and his complete cooperation," she said. "He's written up everything that's happened and kept a diary."

In a handwritten letter from Middleton Jail to prospective writers, Richard Sharpe agreed, at a price, to provide "*exclusive* face-to-face interviews, access to all my medical and/or psychiatric records, family photos and written biographical summaries to questions."

In May, Sharpe called Karen's best friend Connie Behnke out of the blue, inviting her to come and visit him in jail. Saying he was concerned about Mikey and Ali, he asked her how they were doing at their new school in Connecticut and whether they were adjusting properly. Then he asked how often she spoke to Shannon.

"He told me how much he loved Karen," Behnke remembered. "I said that was so bizarre coming from him, and then he said if I wanted to know what happened *that* night, I should come and visit him."

Amazed at what she was hearing, Connie made an excuse and put down the phone.

"He was sitting there wondering, 'How can I get at Shannon?' as he'd exhausted every possibility," reasoned Connie later. "And he thought, 'Well, I wonder if Connie's talking to Shannon.' So he called and it was all about—'Tell me, how are the kids? I miss the kids and I loved Karen so much. By the way, how often do you talk to Shannon?' He was just trying to figure out an angle to get to Shannon."

For the next month Sharpe bombarded Shannon with telephone calls, without getting any response. Finally in July he began to leave threatening messages on her answering machine. Angry and furious at his constant harassment, Shannon complained to Sheriff Frank Cousins Jr., who immediately took action.

"He was put in segregation for using the phone to threaten his daughter," said a prison spokesman, adding that Sharpe would remain in isolation until a disciplinary hearing could be scheduled.

Chapter Twenty-two

THE PROBLEM CHILD

For the rest of the summer, Richard Sharpe mostly stayed in isolation at Middleton Jail, with all his incoming and outgoing telephone calls closely monitored. He dramatically called it "the hole," as if he were a prisoner of war.

He spent a great deal of time discussing tactics for his upcoming trial with Joe and Juliane Balliro and being psychoanalyzed by the high-powered new defense forensic psychiatrist, Keith Ablow. Youthful and genial, the shaven-headed doctor, who specializes in treating violent offenders, is also a best-selling crime novelist, whose hero Frank Clevenger is a forensic psychiatrist.

The defense was pinning a lot of hope on Dr. Ablow, and he spent many hours in Middleton Jail examining Richard Sharpe in the months leading up to the trial.

Originally scheduled for June, the Sharpe trial was first put back to October and then postponed to November, giving attorneys on both sides more time to prepare their cases. Joe Balliro did not underestimate the difficulties he faced in getting a Massachusetts jury to find his client insane. Statistics showed that the insanity defense is only used in one percent of criminal cases, out of which it is only successful in one out of four.

Balliro asked Judge Christine McEvoy to have all prospective jurors fill out a fifty-nine–question survey, ranging from their opinion of cross-dressers to whether they knew of the Sharpe case. The attorney noted that statistics proved that two out of three Americans disapproved of the insanity defense.

"A defendant who asserts that he is not guilty by reason of insanity," wrote Balliro, "faces a jury pool that is hopelessly tainted by public opposition to the defense itself."

But Balliro would soon discover that perhaps his biggest problem would be Richard Sharpe, who, from the very first day of jury selection at Lawrence Superior Court, would play by his own bizarre set of rules. The case had drawn national and international media attention and Court TV planned to cover it gavel-to-gavel. The former doctor would soon turn the courtroom into a circus freak show with his antics.

On Monday, November 5, 2001, one hundred potential jurors filed into the old classic Romanesque-style courthouse. Built in 1860, it dominates the main town green at the corner of Appleton and Common Streets. They squeezed onto long wooden benches in the tiny public gallery to be questioned by Judge McEvoy.

Then Richard Sharpe was led into the court by guards to face charges of first-degree murder, illegal possession of a firearm and breaching a restraining order.

Since his arrest fifteen months earlier, he had grown his dark hair well past his shoulders, and now resembled a badly drawn caricature of rock star Mick Jagger. Dressed in a rumpled dress shirt and necktie, he looked frail, gaunt and sallow, hardly an advertisement for the cosmetic procedures that had made him millions.

During the four-and-a-half-hour–long morning session, Sharpe sat at the defense table for long periods with his eyes shut, often pinching the bridge of his nose or holding his forehead, as if he had a migraine. Occasionally he would whisper something to Joe Balliro, apparently giving his opinion about the usefulness of a potential juror.

Shortly after midday Balliro told Judge McEvoy that Sharpe was feeling unwell and needed the anti-anxiety medication Xanax.

"My client tells me he's experiencing a great deal of anxiety," said Balliro, "and is likely to go into a full panic attack."

After a hasty sidebar with Balliro and Bob Weiner, the assistant Essex County D.A. who would be prosecuting the case, Judge McEvoy asked a court official to call Sharpe's prison doctor to determine if the drug was necessary. Apparently the doctor did not think it was, and Sharpe had to continue without it. During the first grueling day of selection, just two men and two women made the cut, out of the forty-nine who were questioned.

On Tuesday, Sharpe managed to behave himself, as another seven jurors were selected out of a possible fifty, now bringing the total up to six women and five men. But that night, back at Middleton Jail, Sharpe refused to be placed in leg shackles, lashing out physically at a prison guard. Essex House of Correction spokesman Paul Fleming said that Sharpe had started the trouble by pushing an intake officer.

"The intake officer turned him around, put him against a wall, handcuffed him and walked him into our administrative segregation unit," explained Fleming, adding that the prisoner had never complained of any injuries or requested medical attention. "It's a lie. He's been a problem child since he's been here [and] I think inmate Sharpe is just performing for the cameras and the press."

The following morning guards came to his cell to take him to court and found him in the fetal position, refusing to move. He wouldn't get dressed and was eventually brought into the courtroom wearing the standard bright orange prison jumpsuit, shackled at his hands and feet.

Then the final day of jury selection was delayed for the morning, after Joe Balliro told the judge that his client had been roughed up by prison officers the night before, suffering a concussion and other injuries, and was in "desperate need" of medical help.

"He was grabbed by his cuffs, slammed against the wall," stormed the attorney angrily. "His head struck the wall."

Balliro said he was not sure his client was "competent to proceed," explaining that he was in pain and had had no sleep.

Prosecutor Bob Weiner said the accusations were groundless.

"Nothing happened last night," he told Judge McEvoy. "The defendant just refused to come to court this morning, refused to get dressed."

Sharpe was then taken straight to Lawrence General Hospital in an ambulance under armed guard, in case of another escape attempt. There Dr. Patrick Curran took CAT scans, finding only minor injuries to his head and a slight pain in his wrist.

"I did not find anything that would restrict his activity," Dr. Curran testified later that morning when Sharpe was returned to court. As the judge ordered jury selection to resume that afternoon, Sharpe was led out of the courtroom, hurling profanities at a guard sitting by the door.

Judge McEvoy was visibly frustrated by all the holdups when the selection process resumed at 2:00 p.m. The day before she had half-joked that she hardly had any voice left, after individually interviewing more than 150 prospective jurors. Now wearing a pressed dress shirt and tie, Sharpe seemed happier, spending the afternoon session reading over juror questionnaires and even smiling and joking with his attorneys.

That afternoon the remaining five jurors were selected and Judge McEvoy told the final nine women and six men that tomorrow they would tour some of the key sites in the case in a rented coach. Under the Massachusetts legal system all sixteen jurors hear the case and the final twelve are only chosen after closing arguments to begin deliberation. None would know during the actual trial if they would make the final cut.

Trouble struck the trial once again on Thursday, although this time it had nothing to do with the defendant, who had waived his right to view the case sites.

The jurors were taken on a rented bus for the one-hour journey to Gloucester, and first shown Alden Tarr's run-down house at 108 Washington Street. They toured the living room, paying particular attention to the gun rack, where prosecutors alleged Sharpe stole a .30-caliber Weatherby rifle on the night of Karen's murder. From there they went to 8 Great Ledge Lane, where the Sharpe family had lived before Karen left, and where Richard had run his LaseHair and ClickMed businesses.

But then, on the journey to 19 Hull Street, Wenham, retracing Sharpe's murderous steps of July 14, the bus broke down, leaving everybody stranded. Another bus had to be hastily arranged to bring them back to Lawrence, with the judge postponing the Hull Street viewing until Friday morning.

On Friday, November 9, after viewing the murder scene in Wenham, the jurors were driven back to Lawrence

Superior Court for the opening arguments. The Court TV cameras were rolling when Richard Sharpe, looking pale and drawn, was escorted over to the defense table by guards, to take his place between Joe and Juliane Balliro. Wearing a blue shirt and tie, Sharpe nervously sipped water from a beaker as he stroked his long hair, waiting for the trial to begin.

After Judge McEvoy advised the sixteen jurors that the government had the burden of proving that Sharpe was criminally responsible at the time of the murder, Assistant D.A. Robert Weiner presented his opening arguments. The dapper, mustached twenty-three-year veteran of the Essex County D.A.'s Office, who had last crossed swords with Joe Balliro eighteen years earlier when he had prosecuted a motorcycle gang rape trial, was all business as he outlined his case.

"The government expects to prove that this defendant, Richard J. Sharpe, did assault and beat Karen Sharpe with intent to murder her," he began, "and by such assault and beating did kill and murder said Karen Sharpe, a woman to whom he had been married for twenty-seven years.

He outlined how the Sharpes had first met at Shelton High School, fallen in love and married. Sharpe had then become a successful physician, specializing in dermatology, and they'd moved to Gloucester.

"Even more than his medical practice," said Weiner, "the defendant liked business and business ventures and business deals."

Sharpe became visibly animated as the prosecutor began describing his "rocky marriage" and his "hostile relationship" with Karen, that led to her fleeing in March 2000.

"Shortly after her moving out, within days, members of the jury, the defendant filed divorce papers in the probate court here in Essex County. He sought a couple of things. He wanted to terminate the marriage, and he wanted custody of the kids, but the most important thing we will prove to you is that he wanted to get back almost three million dollars that was now in Karen Sharpe's name. Because shortly before she left, the defendant put almost three million dollars in Karen's name because he was expecting to be sued by some Web site company, and he wanted to shelter his assets.

"And he was getting frustrated that he couldn't get the money back. She wouldn't give it back to him and he was getting angry about the money . . ."

At that point Richard Sharpe could no longer contain himself, leaning forward on the defense table, shouting, "I didn't care about the money! It's lies! You're a liar!"

As the whole court seemed to hold its breath at the astonishing outburst, Joe Balliro tried to calm him down.

"Mr. Balliro, will you speak to your client?" said Judge McEvoy, fast losing her patience with Sharpe. "Because if there's another outburst, I'll remove him."

Then Sharpe listened impassionately, his head in his hands and hair falling into his eyes, as Weiner methodically described the circumstances that culminated in Karen's murder, his eighteen hours on the run and the still-missing .22-caliber rifle.

"The defendant may say that he is not criminally responsible for his actions," said Weiner. "But we will prove to you, members of the jury, beyond a reasonable doubt, that this defendant is sane—that this defendant is criminally responsible. He may engage in some socially inadequate behavior, maybe some unorthodox behavior. But that does not equate to insanity."

Then Joe Balliro stood up to present his opening remarks. And he certainly got the court's attention when he began by unleashing a stream of profanities, explain-

ing that these were the same obscenities that Richard
Sharpe's father had hurled at his son every day as he
grew up. He told the jury that his client suffered from
half-a-dozen psychological defects and had only received the most "rudimentary" of treatment.

"This is not a case, ladies and gentlemen, where the
defense is suggesting that he had some temporary kind
of insanity on July 14, that led to the death of his wife,"
explained the veteran trial attorney. "The evidence will
show that it was a condition that had persisted from the
time that he was young."

Warning the jury not to confuse his successful medical career with sanity, Balliro claimed that his client had
been insane for many years.

"The fact that he was a doctor was what led to him
being able to cover it up sufficiently so that he could
otherwise function in society."

Calling it a "rags to riches" story, Balliro sketched
out how self-educated Sharpe had gone on to medical
school, becoming a successful doctor and a millionaire
several times over.

Then he concluded by asking the jury to find Sharpe
not guilty by reason of insanity, saying it would mean
him probably spending the rest of his life in Bridgewater
State Mental Hospital.

As Balliro sat down and conferred with Sharpe, Judge
McEvoy called a one-hour lunch break before the first
prosecution witness would take the stand.

Chapter Twenty-three

THE COMMONWEALTH OF MASSACHUSETTS VS. RICHARD SHARPE

The first witness for the prosecution to take the stand was Kristen Dormitzer, the college sophomore friend of Shannon Sharpe's, who had agreed to babysit Mikey and Ali on the night of the murder. Looking calm and composed, the pretty blonde told how she was about to go to the hospital with Karen, after little Aurora Reagan had accidentally scratched her eye. Suddenly the front door opened and Richard Sharpe poked his head through, meekly asking if Karen was there.

"Karen looked at the man and said, 'Richard, you're not supposed to be here,' " said Dormitzer in hushed tones. "And she took a step towards the door. He pulled a gun from behind his back. He shot her. I saw a kind of an explosion followed by sparks. I felt the heat flash and a smell. I dove out of the way and ran."

Dormitzer then described how she had bravely rescued Mikey and Ali and stayed with them in the bathroom shower praying, until the police arrived.

Watching the riveting testimony from the front row of the public gallery—just ten feet away from Richard Sharpe—was Karen's father John Hatfield, her sister

Kathleen Lembo and Kathleen's husband Victor. For the rest of the trial the Hatfields would find it hard to contain themselves, being in such close proximity to Karen's killer.

"I'm not sure if the guards were there to protect us, or him from us," Karen's dad would later say. "There was a strong temptation to reach over . . . I did this in my mind many times, smashing his head on the table and breaking his back over that railing. But I had to content myself with only doing that in my mind."

The trial resumed on Tuesday, November 13, as Monday was Veterans Day. The next witness was Karen's best friend Connie Behnke, who told the court that she had often seen Richard Sharpe verbally abuse his wife, calling her fat and ugly and telling her to "shut up, because she didn't know what she was talking about."

The housewife and mother of three said that after Karen left him, Sharpe had sought her advice on getting a reconciliation, often becoming angry and accusing Karen of stealing his money. On one occasion, she testified, she had overheard him tell his seven-year-old son Michael, "Your mother stole my money."

On hearing this, there was yet another outburst from Sharpe, who interjected: "I seriously doubt that," and was quickly hushed by a court officer, who told him: "Keep your mouth shut."

The next witness was Jamie Hatfield's former girlfriend Christine Reagan, who had been an eyewitness to Karen's murder. She testified how she had been sitting on a rug in the front foyer when one of the double front doors opened, revealing Sharpe's white, sweaty-looking face.

"He asked me if Karen was home," she told the jury. "And before I could answer, she came around the corner of the kitchen and the door flew completely open and he pulled up a rifle. And that's when he shot her with that gun. It was extremely loud and I saw a bright light. [Karen] fell right where she was standing. All I could think of was that I needed to call 911."

At the start of her cross-examination of Reagan, Juliane Balliro tried to show that Sharpe had been in the throes of madness when he shot his wife. She asked the young woman if she had described the defendant's face as "ghostly" to Sergeant Michael Cronin the day after the murder, but Reagan denied it, saying she had only used the words " 'ghastly' or 'glazed.' "

Balliro asked if it was fair to say that Sharpe looked "dazed," but Reagan disagreed, saying no.

Then Jamie Hatfield dramatically took the stand and told of seeing his brother-in-law standing in the doorway, by the open door. He heard Christine Reagan asking him who he was; and Sharpe replying, "I need to talk to Karen."

"At that point Karen walked towards the door," he said in a shaky voice, fighting back tears. "She said, 'Richie, you need to leave now.' At that point the defendant raised a rifle from behind the closed door. He shot Karen. She fell to the floor . . ."

Jamie broke down in tears, sipping water until he was composed enough to carry on.

"As soon as I saw the gun come up, my attention went to him," he continued. "And then after he shot her, I went towards her and I continued towards the open door."

Thinking fast, Hatfield said he jumped over to the still-open door, slammed it shut and deadbolted it.

"Then I went back to try and save my sister," he sobbed. "I had somebody slide me a cell phone that was

in my overnight bag on the other side of the wall. I
called 911."

Assistant D.A. Weiner asked him what his state of
mind was as his sister lay dying on the floor in front of
him.

"That's a little difficult to describe, the state of mind
I was in," he answered. "But the best I could offer is
that I was very afraid that more people were getting
shot."

Weiner walked over to the prosecution bench to play
the 911 tape on a portable cassette player. Seeing this,
Joe Balliro objected, but Judge McEvoy overruled him.

Everyone in the courtroom then listened in rapt attention as the dramatic tape was played. Richard Sharpe
slouched over on the defense table, his hands over his
eyes so the jurors could not see his reaction.

James Hatfield:	There's been a shooting!
911 Operator:	OK. Let's get somebody there.
James Hatfield:	We need emergency people here and we need officers—the best you have. And the state police. Whatever you have.
911 Operator:	*Inaudible*
James Hatfield:	My girlfriend is on another cell phone right now. We need people out here. We need them here. My sister's been shot. Dr. Richard Sharpe's the shooter. We don't know if he's in the house or not.

911 Operator:	Who is the person who's got the gun?
James Hatfield:	He's not in the house. He is out of the house. She's been shot and she's on the floor. She might be dying in my arms. We need police and fire department. She's been shot. Can you handle this, or do we need to call someone who can handle this?
911 Operator:	*Inaudible*
James Hatfield:	Can you send somebody to the front door, please?
911 Operator:	Hold on.
James Hatfield:	*(Sounding increasingly exasperated)* It's my sister!
911 Operator:	Is it the front door [where] you are talking?
James Hatfield:	The main entrance. You can't miss it.
911 Operator:	Where are you?
James Hatfield:	I'm at the front door of the main entrance. You can't miss it. Please. If you knock on the front door, I'll come to the front door.
911 Operator:	They're coming slowly. How many people are in the house?
James Hatfield:	A total of six or seven people in the house now.

	Call the ambulance! I need an ambulance now!
911 Operator:	It's coming.
James Hatfield:	There's a police officer here now. He's at the front door.
911 Operator:	Was Mr. Sharpe doing the shooting here on the premises?
James Hatfield:	He is not *in* the house. He is *outside* the house. We need a SWAT team here and get an ambulance for my sister, now!
911 Operator:	They're on their way.
James Hatfield:	And the police officers?
911 Operator:	Where was she shot?
James Hatfield:	I don't know where she was shot. I don't know where. It doesn't matter right now.
911 Operator:	What was he driving?
James Hatfield:	I don't know what he was driving. It was maybe a Toyota. Possibly a Toyota. Who knows what he is driving? He's not in the house. He's outside the fucking house! He is outside the house! *(Sobbing and screaming in the background.)*

During the 911 tape, Karen's family was in tears in the public gallery, as were several jurors. But any reaction from Richard Sharpe was impossible to see, as he still had his hand covering his face.

Then Juliane Balliro began cross-examining Karen's still-emotional younger brother, apparently not gauging the huge sympathy he'd generated amongst jurors. She began comparing his testimony to what he'd told Sergeant Cronin, just hours after he'd watched his sister die.

"Were you trying to tell Sergeant Cronin the truth?" she demanded.

Keeping his cool, Hatfield replied that at the time he was still trying to "piece the night together."

She then moved onto the time in the early 1990s when his brother-in-law had hit him for no apparent reason, asking if he'd been acting in a "bizarre manner."

"What do you consider bizarre?" asked Hatfield, visibly becoming annoyed at her line of questioning.

When she continued, asking whether Sharpe had paraded naked in front of the family, Hatfield denied that that had ever happened.

"The truth is you always felt uncomfortable visiting Karen and Richard, because you never knew when Richard would drink too much and he'd go crazy?" she asked.

"No, I don't think that was the case," he replied.

Then, after broaching the subject of Sharpe "dressing as a female," with Hatfield maintaining that he'd only heard about it after Karen's death, Balliro finished her cross-examination, returning to the defense table. As she sat down next to Sharpe, he seemed irritated and appeared to argue with his attorneys.

Paula Hiltz's ex-boyfriend Alden Tarr then took the stand, wearing red-tinted glasses with his gray hair in a crew-cut. Tarr told of how Sharpe had asked him whether he had a gun for sale more than a month before killing Karen.

"He wanted to buy a rifle for home protection and he mentioned he had money in the house," remembered the bushy-mustached Tarr. "I told him I didn't have any for sale."

He then told how his Weatherby hunting rifle was missing from the gun rack the day after the murder, denying that any ammunition had been taken from his locked safe.

In his cross-examination, Joseph Balliro tried to insinuate that a second .22-caliber rifle was also missing, but Tarr denied this.

Sergeant Michael Coleman, a ballistics expert, then took the stand for the prosecution. Coleman's testimony was crucial to Bob Weiner's case to show that Sharpe had premeditated Karen's murder after she had left him. Although the murder weapon had never been found, he needed to show the jury that it was impossible for the defendant to have fired the .22-caliber bullet that killed Karen from the missing .30-caliber Weatherby rifle. Weiner was convinced that Sharpe had managed to obtain a second .22-caliber rifle prior to the murder.

Sergeant Coleman told how he had conducted a thorough investigation of 19 Hull Street after Karen's murder, finding a portion of the bullet that killed her on the living room floor. The bullet was then measured and analyzed under a microscope, confirming that it had been fired from a .22-caliber weapon. Coleman stated it was impossible for the bullet to have been fired from the larger-barreled Weatherby.

After the lunch recess, Massachusetts State Police forensic scientist Paul Zambella took the stand. In gripping testimony he showed the jury the actual bloodstained brown-colored paisley-design dress and white top, both of which had been mounted on display boards, that Karen had been wearing when she'd been gunned down.

Zambella testified that he had carried out orthotolidine tests which revealed Karen's blood on the clothing, as well as the remains of the .22-caliber bullet.

Joe Balliro did not attempt to cross-examine the forensic scientist, and then Judge McEvoy recessed for the day.

At the beginning of the third day of the trial, Judge McEvoy began by admonishing Sharpe before the jury came in. She was furious at his previous outbursts over the past two days.

"If there are any more disruptions, I'm going to have to reconsider whether or not you stay in the courtroom," the judge said. "I don't want to do that. I have not said anything to you in front of this jury because I don't want to highlight your conduct, but if it does occur again, I'm going to excuse the jury, and we're going to deal with it."

After assuring the judge that he understood her warning, Sharpe held his tongue for the rest of the trial, confining his displeasure to scowls and angry glares at witnesses.

The first witness to take the stand on Wednesday was Jacqueline Feeney's boyfriend, Scott Kilman, who had refused Sharpe's offer of $500 to break into Karen's motel room in March.

"I told him no," testified Kilman. "I was just astonished."

The next witness was the former LaseHair president, Richard Fonte, who testified that he had audited the company's records, discovering that Karen had embezzled 30,000 to 40,000 dollars, an accusation that has never been corroborated. He also told of a dinner he'd had with Sharpe, Shannon and Paula Hiltz the night before the murder, and how the defendant had been "intrigued" by his knowledge of tax shelters and off-shore accounts.

"He kidded me," said Fonte. "He said, 'I wish I'd have put my money in the Cayman Islands instead of where I have it now.'"

Weiner then called Paula Hiltz to the stand, giving jurors their first glimpse into the night her boyfriend killed his wife. Admitting that she had shared a bed with the defendant on several occasions, the former LaseHair receptionist said she had accompanied Sharpe to the Halibut Point restaurant in Gloucester on the night of the murder. She said Sharpe had six or seven glasses of wine there before stopping off at her ex-boyfriend Alden Tarr's house, so she could close some windows. She claimed Sharpe had drunk so much that he had trouble walking to the front door when he went in to look at a coffee table.

Sharpe's former medical colleague Dr. Cynthia Bjorlie, who had hoped to write a book on the case, then entered the witness box, saying she had visited Middleton Jail on a number of occasions after his arrest.

"He said that he loved [Karen]," she told Weiner. "That he wished none of this had happened."

Dr. Bjorlie then said Sharpe had spoken about the murder, saying that he had gone to Hull Street to see his children and had not intended to do anything. "But when Karen came to the door," she testified, "he either reached back, or went back, and got the gun. He didn't go on after that."

Dr. Bjorlie then told how Sharpe had asked her if she would be a witness for him, and she had initially agreed. But after he told her he had been "temporarily insane" when he'd shot Karen, Bjorlie said she did not believe him.

"I told him I didn't think he was crazy," she said.

Under cross-examination, Joe Balliro ripped into her, accusing the aspiring author of deliberately misleading

Sharpe about the true intentions of her visits.

"You were looking for fifteen minutes of fame," thundered Balliro. "And to make a little money from this book."

"Maybe," replied Dr. Bjorlie, holding her own.

The veteran lawyer then castigated her for not coming to him first for permission for the series of interviews.

"You didn't think to call me as a professional and see whether or not I approved of you interviewing Dr. Sharpe," roared Balliro, accusing her of exploiting his client's vulnerability in jail. Dr. Bjorlie didn't respond.

The final witness for the prosecution was Essex County Chief Medical Examiner Richard Evans. His colleague, Leonard Atkins, who originally performed the autopsy on Karen Sharpe, had recently suffered a massive stroke. Evans, who took over the case for Atkins, said that, after carefully reviewing all Atkins reports and records, he was satisfied that Karen had died as a result of a gunshot wound to the chest.

Sharpe listened to Evans' gruesome testimony with his head in his hands, as he heard how the .22-caliber bullet he'd fired had ripped through Karen's body, piercing both lungs and severing her spinal cord. Jurors were then shown two grisly pictures from her autopsy, depicting the terrible damage the bullet had caused.

"They may upset some of you . . . but they are relevant," Judge McEvoy first warned the jury. "They are not admitted in any way to upset you or call up any sympathy for the decedent, Karen Sharpe."

At 12:55 p.m. the prosecution rested its case, after calling fifteen witnesses in just three days. But the real drama would begin the next day, with the defense of Richard Sharpe.

Chapter Twenty-four

IN HIS OWN DEFENSE

It was an unseasonably warm November day, with highs expected in the mid-60s, when Joe Balliro strutted into the courtroom to begin his defense. Sitting in the public gallery, directly behind Karen's family, were Dawn Ward and her daughter Sophia, who had flown in from Arizona to support their friend in his time of need. As Sharpe was led into court by guards, he smiled and waved to them, to the disgust of Karen's family.

Richard Sharpe's two brothers, Bob and Ben, and his sister, Laurie, had also traveled to Lawrence that day, to testify on his behalf. As Ben and Laurie waited outside the courtroom, Bob was sworn in as the first defense witness on Thursday morning.

Before asking a single question, Balliro requested that the Court TV cameras be turned off, as the witness did not want his face shown while testifying about their late father's abuse.

"I believe in the freedom of the press," he said. "But the whole world is watching, and to me it's not helping his case or anybody else's."

Sharpe said he had never spoken about his father before, and was just recovering after a major operation.

"It hurts," he told the judge. "Things that happened with my father. I never told anybody about this."

Judge McEvoy then ordered Court TV not to show Bob Sharpe's face as he testified—but it was too late. Millions of viewers had already seen it while he had argued his case for privacy.

Prompted by Balliro, Sharpe told how his father, Benjamin Sharpe, had once viciously attacked him, almost killing him, in front of Richard, as a boy.

"Pop hit me in the head with a poker," he said. "For no reason at all, by the way."

Sharpe said their father verbally abused Richard as a young boy, calling him "stupid" and "worthless."

"He basically wanted to make us feel low," he explained. "My father was unique."

On cross-examination by Bob Weiner, Sharpe said that the whole family had been proud of Richard rising above adversity to achieve success as a doctor.

Then the middle Sharpe brother, Ben, took the stand, describing episodes when Richard would lose his temper, culminating in the 1980 New Year's Eve episode, when Ben threw him out of his restaurant.

"Richard was sometimes a very good person, but he had very bad traits," explained Ben. "He would blow up. He would be very unstable if someone did something he didn't like. He was always on the edge of attack."

Balliro then called a succession of witnesses to show Richard Sharpe's instability, and the high levels of prescription drugs and alcohol he was ingesting on a regular basis. Patricia Duffey, whom he'd hired as a consultant for LaseHair in the spring of 2000, recounted a business lunch during which he suddenly went blank and stared into space. She said it had frightened her, and she'd resolved never to be alone with him again.

Another former LaseHair employee and friend, Jacqueline Feeney, told how she had arrived at Great Ledge Lane the day before Karen left. She'd found Sharpe "curled up in a fetal position," in his bedroom. She also testified how she had joked about his affinity for cross-dressing after he told her about the photographs of him in drag.

"He didn't seem embarrassed about it or anything," she said. "And I didn't want to see them."

Then, Richard Sharpe's sister Laurie Monopoly took the stand. With her straight blonde hair and angular features, Laurie looked uncannily like her brother. She began by telling how Richard had beaten and abused her while they were growing up in Shelton.

Told by Joe Balliro to be explicit in the insults their father had hurled at Richard, Laurie started crying, and wiped her eyes with a handkerchief as she composed herself.

"He put Richard down," she sobbed, "and called him 'a fucking waste,' over and over again."

She said her brother gave as good as he got, calling his father "a fucking this or that."

"It was just very, very violent back and forth, language-wise," she said.

Laurie said Richard always seemed to be jealous of her and she found it very difficult to get along with him, adding that he wasn't a very "enjoyable person" for her to play with as a child. But during his teenage years, she said, he got even "more aggressive" and "more bizarre," frequently attacking their mother, calling her a "scumbag" or a "prostitute."

"She would take the abuse," she explained.

During his sister's testimony, Sharpe listened intently, taking notes and passing suggestions for questions to ask over to Balliro. But as soon as Laurie was dismissed by

Judge McEvoy, Sharpe continued his act of rubbing his eyes and putting his hands over his face, something that was not missed by the Court TV commentators and reporters.

Just after midday, Juliane Balliro suddenly called Richard Sharpe to the stand to testify in his own defense. Everyone in the courtroom gasped and even prosecutor Bob Weiner was taken off guard, as he had not expected the defense to risk putting its unpredictable client on the stand.

Sharpe, wearing a rumpled blue shirt and black tie, with his long dark hair falling over his face, ambled up to the witness box.

"Richard Sharpe," began Juliane Balliro, "we obviously know who you are, but if you could please state your full name for the record?"

"Richard Sharpe," he mumbled flatly.

Guided by Balliro, the defendant began outlining his troubled childhood, surprising many spectators by how articulate and coherent he appeared.

He spoke matter-of-factly of his father's violent abuse, that would "degrade" him with "profanities," noting that he only rarely abused his sister Laurie.

To the point and focused, he related his disturbing story in a monotone, keeping his eyes tightly shut and occasionally brushing his long hair out of his face.

Asked by Balliro exactly what his late father called him, Sharpe replied, " 'worthless bastard,' 'dumb fuck.' I mean, you name it . . . everything . . . every permutation and combination of profanities that you can imagine."

Then, he spoke about how he had begun to crossdress at the age of ten, when he realized that Laurie was never persecuted by their father.

"I felt more relaxed and safer dressed like that," he

said, describing the very first time he bought a female outfit at the age of 14 or 15, and shyly ventured out in public.

"I was *so* convincing," he said proudly, running his long, delicate fingers through his hair.

And then, with Karen's family sitting directly in front of him in the public gallery, he calmly related how he had first met Karen.

"I must have been sixteen or seventeen," he began. "She was about nine, ten or eleven months younger. I actually remember it was the junior year of high school, and I remember fairly clearly what happened."

He sobbed, remembering the first time he set eyes on his future wife at Shelton High and noticed her "built not stuffed" jeans patch. In floods of tears, he spoke of the early days of their relationship and how they would call each other at night, often keeping the line open when they went to sleep.

In December 1972, he said, Karen had become pregnant and they had been pressured by her parents to put the baby up for adoption.

"I started taking care of it," he said. "And I actually started getting serious."

After baby Shannon was born, soon after their graduation, he straightened out his life, married Karen and began studying hard, taking odd-jobs to support the family. The Hatfields bristled with anger as they listened to him taking all the credit for achieving his goal of becoming a doctor, never once mentioning the crucial part Karen had played in financially supporting him.

Asked about "difficulties" during the first years of their marriage, Sharpe blamed Karen. He said she was having an affair which had led to him "slapping her" during an argument. A couple of years later, he said, they had had another fight after Karen accused him of cheating with a woman he had hired to work on a medical project.

"Well, she stomped out, saying she was going to pack up her things and move out because I was cheating on her," he droned. "I tried to go back to work initially. Then I became extremely concerned that she might actually leave."

He then told how he had jumped in his car and refused to stop after a police officer tried to flag him down for going through a stop sign.

"I was so upset about Karen leaving, I just kept going," he said, adding that the police had arrived at their home while he was having a "big blow-out fight" with Karen, and arrested him.

"We had a lot of arguments," he said. "Basically on the average they were about trivial things, and just normal verbal shouting matches. On rare occasions we'd throw things at each other. Only on a few occasions did it become physical."

When Juliane Balliro asked if he and Karen had ever learned to resolve their differences, Sharpe said they hadn't and had never sought counseling.

Throughout his hours on the stand, Sharpe had to keep being reminded by Judge McEvoy and Juliane Balliro to stop mumbling, as he often could not be heard by the jury. "I know it's difficult," Balliro told him halfway through the afternoon, "but could you try and keep your voice up so the court reporter and all the jurors can hear your testimony?"

When Juliane Balliro asked him about his 1991 involuntary committal to the Arbour Hospital and stabbing Karen with a fork, Sharpe glossed over it.

"At some point I picked up a fork and swung it at her and scratched her forehead," he claimed. "She said I was incoherent."

Failing to mention how he had blackmailed Karen into withdrawing her original statement about his vicious assault on her with the fork, he now claimed it had been her idea, because she wanted him home. And according to Sharpe, after being released from the Arbour, he had considered divorcing Karen, concerned that she was using him as a "meal ticket" and did not love him.

"I tended to be a little paranoid at times," he admitted.

When Balliro asked him about his family life after the births of Mikey and Ali, Sharpe visibly brightened, once again recounting his rose-colored version of being a perfect father.

"We were a real family," he claimed. "Karen would meet me with the two kids, and things were as good as they'd ever been. And they were getting better."

Then, after two hours of direct examination, Judge McEvoy called an afternoon recess. Sharpe returned to the defense table to get some feedback about his performance thus far.

On his return to the stand twenty minutes later, Juliane Balliro led him through the circumstances that culminated in Karen's murder, beginning with her walking out in early March, "within two days" of him transferring $2.9 million and the Wenham house into her name.

"I was scared," he stammered, clenching his eyes shut as if in pain. "I felt confused."

To survive the shock of losing his wife, he told Balliro, he "upped" his dose of tranquilizers, describing himself as "an emotional wreck."

When Balliro brought up the subject of Karen's contractor, Marc Beauregard, Sharpe became agitated, saying she had "secretly hired a contractor," and he had only found out about the affair after overhearing some workmen talking about their boss "porking some rich bitch in Wenham."

But he became even angrier when Balliro asked him about Jacob Atwood, and their face-to-face meeting at a probate court hearing.

"Atwood filed a bunch of affidavits, accusing me of everything from going around in slinky skirts twenty-four hours a day to alcohol and drug abuse. Physical abuse," Sharpe declared. "And when I was in the bathroom, I was accosted violently, and he said, 'A fag transvestite like you shouldn't have kids.' Whatever compensational ability I had, I lost that day. I just couldn't deal with any of this."

He then described his accident, falling down a flight of stairs carrying a heavy laser and breaking his pelvis, happily spelling out the cocktails of drugs he was prescribed in the hospital.

"Initially I was treated with Demerol, which is a narcotic pain reliever," the doctor explained. "Then I was changed to Percocet, with is an oral narcotic. At some point, I'm not sure when, I believe my doctors suggested [an anti-depressant], because I had increasing anxiety and depression. I was put on Celexa, an anti-depressant, and I was also put on Altrium, which is a barbiturate-like pain reliever and a muscle relaxant for my back. I think that was it."

Then he claimed that it had been Scott Kilman's idea to break into Karen's motel room. "I told Scott I was going to stake out the place myself," claimed Sharpe. "He tried to talk me out of it."

At this point Judge McEvoy broke for the day, telling the jury to be back at 9:00 a.m. the following morning, when the defendant would resume testifying. As Sharpe was handcuffed and returned to Middleton Jail, he knew that tomorrow's line of questioning by Bob Weiner would be anything but the cakewalk he had enjoyed today.

Chapter Twenty-five

"YOU WANTED TO KILL
KAREN SHARPE!"

At 5:40 a.m. on Friday, November 16, Essex County Correctional Officer Sean Hennessey went to cell #156 at Middleton Jail to wake up Inmate Richard Sharpe. The officer asked prisoner #3445 if he would like a shower before his big day in court, and he said yes, requesting a comb, a toothbrush and some toothpaste. Officer Hennessey waited outside the cell.

When Sharpe realized he was going to be handcuffed, he announced he would not be going to court today.

"At that time I called 120 control and relayed this information to Lieutenant St. Pierre," Officer Hennessey would later note in his official report. "Officer Cronin and I went to cell #156 and explained to Sharpe that he would be going to court today, and he would be handcuffed and shackled. Sharpe again stated he was too stressed."

A few minutes later, Lieutenant St. Pierre arrived to have a word with the problem inmate, who started swearing loudly at him. Finally, after a great deal of swearing and arguing, Sharpe agreed to be handcuffed and shackled, but refused to take a shower or eat any breakfast.

It was well after 9:00 a.m. when Richard Sharpe was finally brought into the Lawrence Superior Courtroom to resume his testimony. No mention of Sharpe's behavior that morning was made by either the defense or the wayward defendant.

Before resuming where they had left off the day before, Juliane Balliro asked Sharpe about a gun incident in the late 1970s, involving his brother Ben. In some last-minute attempt to provide a rationale for killing Karen, his attorney wanted to highlight an incident when Ben Sharpe had taken a gun along to confront a man he suspected was having an affair with his wife.

"I went with him to borrow a handgun from a friend and confronted the [man]," he explained, adding that it ended peaceably.

Then Balliro got the court's full attention, asking him about his fondness for women's clothes. Sharpe said he had cross-dressed at least a couple of hundred times, mostly wearing assorted women's undergarments. He admitted often stealing his daughter Shannon's underwear, saying her clothes fitted him better than Karen's.

"Sometimes I'd just sort of get out of the shower and throw Karen's robe on," he explained, stroking his long, thick hair. "So I guess I was cross-dressing then. I'd sit on the computer and work on Web sites or do paperwork. Sometimes Karen and I would play around, you know."

Then Balliro walked over to a large blank paper tacked onto a blackboard in front of the jury, and began writing, "Emotionally Disturbing Events."

One by one she took Sharpe through his problems, which had combined, she said, to drive him to insanity on the night he killed Karen. Then she dramatically wrote each point down with a black Sharpie pen, as she went through them with him.

1) Losing Family—End of Feb. 2000
2) Disappointment/Betrayal
3) Business Nightmares
4) Broken Bones/Concussion
5) Pneumonia
6) Harassment By Jacob Atwood
7) Loss of Savings
8) Restraining Order
9) Mark [sic] Beauregard
10) Jealousy and Money to MB
11) Medications—5 or 6

"I think Marc Beauregard drove me nuts," he explained at one point, wiping his eyes, while Balliro wrote down each problem. "And this whole idea that he was over there with *my* kids in *our* house that we were going to retire in. And I couldn't go over there. All the stuff, the money, the jealousy."

Moving onto the night of the murder, Balliro concentrated on the alcohol and five or six prescription drugs he had ingested that evening.

"They would make me drowsy," he replied, when asked about the effect of the medicines on his mental state. "They would definitely have an effect."

Sharpe then admitted only stealing the Weatherby rifle and some ammunition from Alden Tarr's house while he was there with Paula Hiltz. This despite the fact that both Tarr and Hiltz had testified all ammunition was safely locked in his basement safe, so her small son could not get hold of it.

When Balliro asked him how the ammunition had gotten into the rifle that he took to 19 Hull Street, he meekly replied, "I think I put it in."

Fighting back tears, he said he walked up to the front double doors and opened one.

"Somebody said, 'You shouldn't be here.' It was a male voice," he said almost inaudibly, his hands covering his face. "Then Karen said she was going to call the police and held up a piece of paper. I thought [it] was a restraining order."

Prompted to tell what happened next, Sharpe sobbed, "The gun going off. I heard the gun go off. I think the noise woke me up a little bit. Then I left."

Finally, Juliane Balliro asked what had been going through his mind during the seven-minute drive from Gloucester to the Wenham house.

"I just wanted my family back," he sighed. "I just wanted to talk to [Karen]."

At about 11:45 a.m., after a short recess, prosecutor Robert Weiner finally got his chance to question Richard Sharpe. Going straight on the attack, he immediately asked about how Sharpe had given Karen "a pretty good slap," soon after they had married, and about his verbal abuse.

"It was a controlled slap," maintained the defendant defiantly. "I would occasionally call Karen names."

Rising to his task, Weiner asked if he had ever called Karen dumb, fat and stupid. Sharpe became evasive, saying he might have.

"And you don't like fat, do you?" asked the assistant D.A. "You remove fat from your own body. And you fit into your daughter's clothes better than your wife's. Isn't that what you testified to?"

"I think it was," replied Sharpe meekly.

Then questioning him about his success with the medical board examinations, Weiner pointedly asked, "You're a pretty smart fellow, aren't you?" to which Sharpe replied, "It depends on how you define smart."

Weiner swiftly went over the history of his violent

abuse against Karen, pointing out the injuries he had given her, including a cut lip, a loose tooth and the 1991 fork-stabbing episode.

"Do you think you were temporarily insane then?" asked the prosecutor.

"I don't know," came the weak reply.

"What about when you slammed her in the seventies? Were you temporarily insane then?"

"I don't know. All these things were in the heat of jealousy or suspected jealousy. I don't know."

Then Weiner questioned the defendant's credibility on the stand, forcing him to admit lying, under oath, to the Massachusetts Board of Registration every time he had to reapply for his medical license, by claiming that he had never had any psychiatric problems.

"You don't think much about the oath that you take, do you, Dr. Sharpe?" asked Weiner, looking straight at the sixteen members of the jury.

"I actually do," countered Sharpe, "but I was lying on that occasion."

Weiner then walked up to the eleven-point list of Sharpe's extenuating circumstances that Juliane Balliro had left behind as a reminder to the jury, aggressively mentioning each one and ticking it off with his forefinger.

When he reached "Loss of Savings," Sharpe claimed the money had been trivial in comparison to the loss of Karen and his family.

"It didn't bother you at all that you had signed over 2.9 million dollars to Karen in February 2000 and she didn't give it back?" asked Weiner incredulously.

"That was an issue," agreed Sharpe. "The major issue was getting my family back. I thought it was evil. I was ready to give it away. And money didn't matter. Only my family mattered."

The prosecutor then switched gears, asking Sharpe

about his foiled escape attempt with fellow inmate Steven Smith.

"You hatched a plan to try and escape?" thundered Weiner.

And in perhaps *the* pivotal moment of the trial, Sharpe opened his eyes and looked straight at the jury, with a well-rehearsed answer at the ready.

"About that time I learned that even if I was found not guilty, I would spend my life in Bridgewater," he declared, shaking with emotion. "So, yes I did. Even if I was found not guilty I'd spend the rest of my life locked up in a psych hospital."

It was a cunning move by Sharpe. And his almost subliminal message that, even if he was found not guilty by reason of insanity, he was not going to go free would later resonate in the jury deliberation room.

"I think he sat there waiting in my cross-examination for the opportune moment," Weiner would later say. "You cannot unring a bell. Once it chimes, it rings in your ear."

The prosecutor then moved to the night of Karen's death, questioning Sharpe about taking the .30-caliber Weatherby from Tarr's house. Then, although Weiner had not yet mentioned the second .22-caliber weapon, Sharpe unwittingly brought it up himself.

"Some people say it was a .22," he intoned. "Some people said it was that or something like that. I don't know."

Then after getting an increasingly evasive Sharpe to admit he "must" have loaded the rifle that would kill Karen, Weiner took the jury on every winding turn of his late-night drive from 8 Great Ledge Lane to the long 338-foot driveway leading to the front door of 19 Hull Street, with the loaded rifle in his hand.

"Are you telling us," demanded Weiner, "for some

reason that because your brother took a gun to some motel when he thought his wife was cheating on him, and nobody got hurt, that in your mind it was OK for you to take that gun to 19 Hull Street?"

"I'm not telling you anything in that regard," snapped Sharpe. "That's up to the experts to decide."

"That's not what was going through your mind," pressed the prosecutor, his voice rising with each question.

"I don't know what the hell was going through my mind. I really don't."

"Well you took a loaded rifle to 19 Hull Street, right? Were you going hunting?" asked Weiner sarcastically, now standing just a few inches away from Sharpe, staring him straight in the eyes.

"You went up there because you wanted to kill Karen Sharpe, didn't you? Dr. Sharpe?"

"I loved Karen," he sobbed.

"You wanted to kill her, didn't you?"

"No, I didn't."

The prosecutor then described how Sharpe had opened the door, poking his head through expecting to see Karen and Marc Beauregard together. Instead, he saw the young babysitter Kristen Dormitzer, and had asked for Karen, who stepped into his view, telling him he wasn't supposed to be there, and tried to shoo him out.

But that was not how Richard Sharpe remembered it.

"I seem to remember her saying something like, 'I'll have you arrested,' " he said through his hands, "and shaking a restraining order or a piece of paper. She was holding a restraining order maybe. I don't know exactly."

"And you were pretty upset at that point, weren't you?" asked Weiner.

"I was upset for months," he whined.

"You were angry, weren't you?"

"I don't think so. I was overrun mostly by sadness."

"Were you angry that night when you walked up to her doorway with that rifle?"

"I honestly don't think so. I mean, I honestly don't think so."

"You think you were just calm and cool and collected?"

"No, I don't know what I was. I was not in a normal state. I was in . . ."

"And you reached back and you picked up the gun and you fired the gun at Karen Sharpe. Didn't you? Didn't you, Dr. Sharpe?"

"Yes."

"And when you shot Karen Sharpe, she fell right here where she stood, didn't she?" said Weiner, as he thrust an autopsy picture of Karen's body right in his face.

"I don't know," sobbed Richard Sharpe. "I turned and walked away."

On Monday, November 19, the sixth day of Richard's trial, the defense psychiatrist, Dr. Keith Ablow, took the stand to attempt to explain the defendant's mental problems in layman's terms. The polished and highly articulate 39-year-old forensic psychiatrist said he had been called in by Joe Balliro eleven months earlier to examine Sharpe, and ascertain his mental condition when he killed his wife. Dr. Ablow told the court that he had spent approximately one hundred hours working on the Sharpe case, including eleven interviews with him in Middleton Jail.

Calling Richard Sharpe "The Perfect Storm," Dr. Ablow testified that he suffered from "numerous" mental disorders, including intermittent explosive disorder, major depression, alcohol-related disorder, borderline personality, obsessive-compulsive disorder and narcissism.

"He has so little in the way of a personal identity and ego strength," said Dr. Ablow, "that he has to go and get them."

Ablow explained that Sharpe both idealized and devalued Karen, and she was the only thing keeping his psychological world intact. When she left him, he completely disintegrated.

"He's used her since age seventeen to stay quasi-normal—or to look that way," said the psychiatrist. "He's really needed her."

Calling him a "victim of severe child abuse," Dr. Ablow said that Sharpe had no real self-identity or ego and displays "very dramatic" symptoms.

"I mean, he's not even comfortable with his gender," he said. "And that's part of your identity. Are you masculine or feminine? Man or woman? He's comforted by the opposite gender, or trappings of it—dressing as a woman.

"He's not sure if he likes his face, and so he has four separate plastic surgeries to alter it. He's not sure of a lot of things about himself. He removes the hair from his body. But the cross-dressing, and the fact that he's comforted by it, is a very dramatic symptom of identity disturbance."

The psychiatrist said that Richard Sharpe's entire life had been one long attempt to appear normal. And he was only able to carry off the charade because of his high intelligence, coupled with his professional success as a doctor and businessman.

Turning to the murder, Dr. Ablow testified that Sharpe entered into a dissociative state on the night of July 14, when he drove to Wenham and shot Karen Sharpe.

"He entered this place," explained Dr. Ablow. "He was having these insistent thoughts to *go home*. He wasn't even sure what that meant, and he did things that showed he had lost contact with reality."

When he pulled the trigger, killing Karen, Dr. Ablow said, Sharpe "very likely couldn't tell right from wrong," highlighting the very basis of an insanity defense.

Prosecutor Bob Weiner strongly challenged the doctor's diagnosis, citing the opinion of forensic experts who proved Karen was killed with a .22-caliber rifle and not a .30-caliber bullet from the stolen Weatherby, as Sharpe had testified.

Weiner then asked Dr. Ablow if his diagnosis would change "If the defendant already had a .22-caliber rifle and took the .30-caliber rifle to make it look like the killing was spur-of-the-moment?"

"Maybe," Dr. Ablow replied.

While Dr. Ablow was testifying, Karen Sharpe's estate filed a wrongful death suit against Alden Tarr Jr. and his parents, Alden Sr. and Priscilla. The suit, lodged in Salem Superior Court, alleged wrongful death, wanton and reckless conduct and negligence.

"As a result of the negligent storage of such weapons and the ability of Richard Sharpe to access such weapons," read the suit, "Karen Sharpe was murdered on or about July 14, 2000."

On Tuesday, November 20, the prosecution called its own psychiatrist, Dr. Malcolm Rogers, as a rebuttal witness, who said that, although Richard Sharpe might suffer from a personality disorder, making him arrogant and deceitful, he was not insane when he killed his wife. The associate clinical professor of psychiatry at Harvard Medical School testified on rebuttal that the defendant knew right from wrong when he pulled the trigger.

"My opinion is he was able to weigh the pros and cons of his actions," he declared.

Sharpe, Dr. Rogers testified, was in control of himself on July 14, making decisions and having dinner and dancing with his girlfriend Paula Hiltz, only hours before the murder.

"He made choices," said the psychiatrist. "[He] made business decisions. He was able to do that in a way that was in his best interest."

Rogers said the mere fact that Sharpe had fled Massachusetts and gotten rid of the weapons proved "he had the capacity to appreciate wrongfulness."

"In my opinion, the defendant did not have a mental disease or defect at the time that prevented him from conforming his behavior to the requirements of the law," he said.

Dr. Rogers was the final witness in the seven-day trial, and several jurors looked bored and were fidgeting during his lengthy testimony. At 3:18 p.m. the defense rested its case.

Earlier that week, Judge McEvoy had balloted the sixteen jurors to see if they wanted to hear closing arguments tomorrow and then deliberate over the upcoming Thanksgiving holiday, or come back next week. Not surprisingly, the unanimous decision was to take a well-deserved break from the trial.

"At your request, and at the request of the attorneys," said Judge McEvoy, "we will adjourn until Monday morning. And [then] we will proceed with the closing arguments. You may not discuss the case with anyone. Please put it out of your minds and enjoy yourself with the holiday. Enjoy your time off with your families and your friends. And stay healthy so you can return on Monday morning."

Chapter Twenty-six

"THE WINNER WAS JUSTICE"

On Monday morning there was tension in the Lawrence courtroom, as well an air of expectancy, as prosecutor Robert Weiner and defense attorney Joseph Balliro prepared for Judge McEvoy to take her seat for the closing arguments. The two opponents had had almost a week to fine-tune their final addresses to the jury, before twelve would be selected and sequestered until they made a unanimous decision.

Richard Sharpe seemed agitated and apprehensive, as he made last-minute suggestions to Balliro. Karen's family, sitting at their usual place in the public gallery, looked tired and drained from the emotional toll the trial had taken.

Then Judge Christine McEvoy took her seat and began with a warning to everyone to keep quiet during the closing arguments, saying she would not tolerate any outbursts.

"This cannot happen," she declared, looking straight at Sharpe. "Have you understood that?"

Under Massachusetts law, unlike other states, it is the defense who presents its closing arguments first. So Joe

Balliro stood up to address the jury, immediately accusing the prosecutor of amateur dramatics.

"It may make good television," he said. "But it doesn't help you one bit if it enflames your emotions and your passions."

The veteran attorney then told the jury that Richard Sharpe walked a tightrope between genius and insanity.

"You remember that all through history there have been people who were crazy as a loon, who ran countries, who planned all kinds of things but were *totally* insane. Going back to the time when Nero was fiddling while Rome was burning."

Emphasizing that it was not a "battle of psychiatrists," Balliro told the jury that Sharpe was "about as crazy, about as insane as anyone you would ever meet." Continuing, he said that if a homeless person had done onetenth of what Sharpe had, he would be locked up forever.

"The difference was his intelligence," said the attorney. "The fact that he's a doctor."

Finishing up, Balliro suggested that Richard Sharpe went to Wenham on July 14 just to be near his family.

"He thought he was going home," he said. "And in his disoriented, dissociative state, in his fantasy, he *was* going home. I suggest that we have proven overwhelmingly that on July 14, 2000, he was insane within the legal definition. And that the verdict in this case is not guilty by reason of insanity."

Then Bob Weiner delivered his closing argument. He began by saying that the "centerpiece" of the defense's insanity case consisted of "parading" the siblings in front of the jury.

"I submit to you child abuse is no excuse," he said. "Members of the jury, you cannot return a verdict in this case based on sympathy for the defendant because he may have been abused as a child, any more than you can return a verdict of guilty of first-degree murder based on sympathy and the fact that he abused Karen Sharpe and killed her."

Weiner also said that "cross-dressing does not equal insanity," and it is not an excuse, any more than Sharpe's attempt to grow breasts was.

"I submit to you there were three million motives that Richard Sharpe had for killing Karen," he thundered. "He was infuriated about the money. He couldn't stop talking about the money. Not how much he wanted her back. He wanted the money back.

"You may have seen *Jerry Maguire*, what's [Cuba Gooding, Jr.] say? 'Show me the money!' That's his motive here."

And then Weiner told jurors that Richard Sharpe had been putting on a calculated act for them throughout the trial, attempting to make himself appear crazy.

"It's called malingering," said Weiner, looking directly at Sharpe, who sat grimacing at the defense table. "He's faking it. He's trying to fake symptoms for secondary gain. Because he wants to develop a temporary insanity case. That's what he's doing, members of the jury. I submit to you that he was perceptive and manipulative in trying to fabricate this defense of temporary insanity.

"Now Your Honor is going to tell you what deliberate premeditation is. The law recognizes how quickly the human mind can work. We don't have to prove that the defendant planned this murder for months. The law recognizes that you can create that plan in a matter of weeks, days, hours, minutes and even seconds.

"When he went to that house at 19 Hull Street he had every intention of killing Karen Sharpe. He had weighed the pros and cons of his actions and he knew what he was going to do and he did it. And I suggest to you, members of the jury, that a true verdict in this case is one of the highest degree of murder—murder in the first degree. And the defendant committed that murder in the first degree and should be held criminally responsible for it. And I thank you for your attention and attendance at this trial."

After lunch, Judge McEvoy instructed the jurors on the different verdicts they would be considering. Under Massachusetts law, she told them that first-degree murder was the unlawful killing of a human being with malice and deliberate premeditation. But in second-degree murder, although malice is an element, premeditation is not. Second-degree murder is defined as an intent to cause death or grievous bodily harm, or an act that any reasonable person would have known would result in death. The judge said that the jury should only consider a verdict of manslaughter if they decided that the state had not met the burden of proof for murder in either the first or second degree.

She then briefed them on the legal requirements of finding Richard Sharpe insane, and whether he lacked criminal responsibility when he killed Karen Sharpe.

Said the judge: "If you establish beyond a reasonable doubt that the defendant committed the crime, you must decide whether the Commonwealth has met the additional burden of proof of criminal responsibility."

Pointing out that, although a defendant can be competent to stand trial today, he may not be criminally responsible for previous offenses, the judge continued, "Criminal responsibility is a legal term. A person is not criminally responsible for his or her conduct if he or she has a mental disorder or defect, and as a result of that mental disease or defect, lacked substantial capacity either to appreciate the criminality or wrongfulness of his or her conduct to the requirements of the law."

Then the jurors left the courtroom and the four alternates were selected. The remaining six men and six women started deliberating the fate of Richard Sharpe at 3:30 p.m.

That night the jurors had still not reached a decision and were sequestered at a local hotel. A female juror would later remember feeling overwhelmed when she was first locked in the jury room, having no idea what her decision would be.

Deciding not to take a vote right away, the jurors sifted through all the evidence and the law. Some jurors felt sympathy for the childhood abuse Sharpe had suffered, while others didn't. But most agreed that Sharpe had damned himself by taking the stand, allowing them to see the method of his madness. At the end of the first day they were divided as to whether he was insane or not.

On Tuesday morning, Shannon Sharpe made her first appearance in the courtroom since her father's trial began, arriving with Karen's family. They spent the day huddled in the courtroom anxiously awaiting a verdict. The family were angry and frustrated about the way the defense had portrayed Karen, as an adulteress and embezzler. They felt hurt that the jury had been given such a distorted picture, such defamation about the sweet, loving mother, daughter and sister they had loved so much.

"We had to listen to all *that* stuff," said her sister Kathleen. "How can they allow these people to say these things and she's not there to defend herself?"

That afternoon, as Richard Sharpe was being escorted by guards along a corridor at the court, he saw Shannon, who happened to be standing there. He began shouting, trying desperately to get her attention. But she turned and walked out, as the guards restrained her father. Badly shaken up by the encounter, she left immediately and returned to New York with her fiancé Wayne Cohen, to await the verdict.

The atmosphere in the courtroom was tense as lawyers and journalists awaited the verdict. Even seasoned prosecutor Bob Weiner looked concerned that it was taking so long, worrying that perhaps the jury had bought into Sharpe's courtroom antics and would declare him insane. "The longer they're out, you never know what's going to happen," said Weiner.

Richard Sharpe spent the day in his cell below the courtroom, curled up in the fetal position.

Then at 6:33 Tuesday night there was a loud knock on the jury door, signaling a verdict, after more than eleven-and-a-half hours of deliberations.

As soon as the word got out, everyone rushed back into the courtroom. There was a stunned silence as the press took their seats, notebooks at the ready, and Karen Sharpe's family and friends packed the public gallery, anxiously awaiting the decision.

Richard Sharpe stood at the defense table displaying no emotion whatsoever, carefully watched by two prison guards, handcuffs at the ready. Then Judge McEvoy took her seat at the head of the court, and the clerk asked jury foreman Alfred Adam if the defendant was guilty or not guilty.

"Guilty of murder in the first degree," said Adam, to gasps and sighs of relief from the public gallery. Sharpe, realizing that the sentence was a mandatory life without parole, jerked his head up-and-down in shock, as the guards rushed forward to handcuff him. Then the foreman pronounced him guilty of possessing a rifle without a license and violation of a restraining order.

After the verdict, the jurors were permitted to sit down as the judge thanked them, setting a sentencing hearing for Thursday. A couple of female jurors, who were still shaking, glared at the surprisingly stoic defendant as he was led away, loudly proclaiming his love for Karen and his kids to the television cameras. A tearful but jubilant Kathleen Lembo hugged Bob Weiner. Later she would explain that the family would have "feared for our lives" if Sharpe had been found not guilty by reason of insanity, as there would then have been a good chance that he might get out one day.

"If this man ever walked the streets again, we would have to disappear," she said. "We wanted him to go to jail forever, as we'd never have been able to raise his children with that hanging over our heads."

Outside the court, at a hastily called press conference, Kathleen Lembo read a prepared statement to the press.

"Karen Sharpe was a loving mother in spite of what anybody says," she asserted. "She was a wonderful daughter and a friend. And that's who she was. You got to hear a lot of things that weren't Karen Sharpe in the courtroom, unfortunately."

Then asked by a reporter how Mikey and Ali were doing, Lembo said they were doing great.

"We're providing them with a loving home and we have a lot of family support. Karen knew what she was living and she also knew that she couldn't escape. She didn't share that with any of us, because she didn't want us to have to feel her pain. It was devastating to the family to find out those things."

Then a victorious, but tired-looking, Bob Weiner addressed the media, calling Karen Sharpe a classic battered woman, who was trying to protect her family from the "pain and agony" she endured over almost three decades.

"There were only really a few people who knew what was going on in the family household," he said. "And it was only at the end that she was free of the yoke of Richard Sharpe, but unfortunately it was too late. But it was her new-found freedom from Richard Sharpe that ultimately caused her death."

Joseph Balliro told reporters that there were no winners in the case.

"This has been a tragedy for everyone," he said sadly, wiping his brow. "Those three children have lost their mother, and now they've lost their father."

Two days later, Kathleen Lembo would angrily allude to Balliro's comments, saying, "Contrary to what the defense attorney has stated, we do believe there was a winner here. The winner was justice."

On Thursday morning Judge Christine McEvoy sentenced Richard Sharpe to spend the rest of his life doing hard labor at the Massachusetts Correctional Institution at Cedar Junction, without the possibility of parole. He also received two-and-a-half years for violating a restraining order and not less than four years, and not more than five years, for illegal possession of a firearm. The sentences were to run concurrently.

Looking genuinely moved, Judge McEvoy then commended the Hatfield family for being so "dignified," while having to sit through such difficult testimony. Then she ordered Sharpe to stand up to formally receive his life sentence.

"I say to you, sir, that this jury has found you to be criminally responsible, and this court now holds you criminally responsible, for the murder of Karen Sharpe. The mandatory sentence of life without parole will be imposed.

"I do feel that this punishment is the just punishment

for what you have done—for murdering your wife. You are committed.

"Recess the court, please."

As the judge returned to her chambers and the courtroom cleared, Richard Sharpe, who had been expecting to address the court, as was his legal right, lashed out. His eyes wildly roamed the emptying courtroom, as bailiffs handcuffed him. But then he suddenly swung around towards the Court TV cameras.

"I have the right to talk," he shouted, tears streaming down his face, as Joe Balliro tried to hush him up. "I loved Karen!"

Then guards dragged him out of the courtroom in leg irons to begin serving his life sentence, screaming, "I'm sorry, I'm sorry."

The next day, in her first interview with the press since the trial, Shannon Sharpe likened her childhood growing up with Richard Sharpe as "like living with a terrorist." The 28-year-old former laser technician, who had just started a new job in New York and was planning her wedding, said she was not surprised by Sharpe's outburst at his sentencing, and could have predicted it.

"I knew that once he didn't have to put an act on for the jury, he would try to speak to me and get the last word in," she told *The Boston Globe*.

EPILOGUE

In the days after Richard Sharpe's sentencing, there was a sense of closure for Karen's family, as they tried to move on from the nightmare and return to a normal life. Mikey and Ali, who were aware of their father's trial, had now settled down and were happy living with the Lembos and their two young daughters.

In December, a month after Richard Sharpe started serving his sentence in the Walpole Penitentiary, it was reported that he had settled the wrongful death suit brought by Karen Sharpe's estate, agreeing to pay her family $5 million. Under the terms of the settlement, Mikey, now 8, and Ali, now 5, would receive what is left of their father's fortune, which had reportedly dwindled to just $1.9 million, out of which $600,000 is owed to lawyers, including $175,000 to Sharpe's defense team.

So far the family's civil suit against Alden Tarr Jr. remains unresolved, although in March 2002, Kristen Dormitzer dropped her action against Sharpe's estate, saying she wanted Mikey and Ali to receive all the money. But the blonde ex-student decided to use her fifteen minutes of fame from the murder trial to embark on a modeling career. She found an agent in Florida and adopted the professional name of Christiane, explaining in her biography how she had been a witness to a "highly publicized murder" and she had appeared in newspapers and television.

"I had been contacted by several modeling scouts who encouraged me to turn a bad situation into something more positive," said her modeling bio. "That is now what I am doing."

But if the family hoped that Sharpe would now disappear from their lives, they were wrong. In March 2002, from behind bars at Walpole, he was accused of hatching an audacious plot to murder Essex County Assistant D.A. Robert Weiner, whom he now apparently blamed for his life sentence. He offered a fellow inmate $100,000 to take out a hit on the prosecutor, but instead the prisoner alerted jail authorities. Sharpe was immediately placed in solitary confinement as the jail launched a full investigation, and later charged in Norfolk County with soliciting a fellow inmate to kill the prosecutor.

A few days later, on Saturday, March 30, Sharpe tried to hang himself with his shoelaces. He was then admitted to the New England Medical Center in critical but stable condition, prompting suspicions that it was another ploy to get moved to a less secure prison environment.

The family still feared he might escape and come after them. "The nightmare never ends," said Kathleen Lembo. "It's just something that we have to deal with."

Shannon Sharpe, who only heard the news when she was called by a reporter for comment, was said to be "terrified" that her father planned to escape and kill his family.

"We're really frightened of him," she told *Boston*

Herald reporter Tom Farmer. "He'll never, as long as he lives, stop trying to harm people."

In late August 2002, a 39-year-old New Jersey nurse named Debbie Keiser-Myers revealed that Richard Sharpe had almost talked her into marriage from behind prison bars. In an emotional interview with the *Boston Herald*, the attractive single woman admitted that she had watched his trial on Court TV and felt so sorry for him that she had written him a letter of sympathy. Sharpe immediately replied and began courting her with a series of sexually charged letters and collect telephone calls, where he declared his undying love.

In his letters he ridiculed his insanity defense, admitting it was merely an act to allow him to serve out his time in the comparative comfort of a mental hospital.

"As part of my defense strategy," he wrote on January 25, 2002, "my 'brilliant lawyer' tried to make me look crazy, out of control, violent, on the verge of a sex-change operation, etc. Not only did the strategy fail, but it neutralized most of the sympathy that I might have gotten otherwise."

He went on to explain that although some women like Keiser-Myers had shown "sympathy," all the cross-dressing publicity had turned "macho males" against him.

"Well, fuck it," wrote Sharpe. "Any male who isn't comfortable in fishnet stockings, spiked heels and a leather miniskirt can go to hell!"

In February he mulled over the possibilities of their future relationship if he could engineer a move to Bridgewater State Mental Hospital, which would allow "contact visits."

"Can you visit and let me kiss you?" he wrote her. "I

really want to just tear clothes off of you and make passionate love to you."

In another letter soon afterwards, he considered undergoing a sex change so he would be transferred out of Walpole to the women's prison in Framingham.

"It might be worth it," he mused. "It would also generate a lot of publicity for the book–movie. If I go this route and then get out of prison, would you consider having a lesbian relationship with me?"

A few weeks later, when Keiser-Myers visited him in Bridgewater State Mental Hospital after his failed suicide attempt, Sharpe asked her to marry him, suggesting he officially propose on national television during an upcoming *Dateline NBC* one-hour special on his case, currently in production.

"He was all over me, kissing me, until the guards screamed at him," she said.

The nurse finally broke off their six-month relationship in the summer when she realized he was just playing games with her and she owed $1,000 in collect telephone calls. Now, she told the *Boston Herald*, she was coming forward so he would not be able to dupe any more gullible women.

"He's that smooth," she explained. "He goes for sympathetic, compassionate women. [I] thought I could help him."

During earlier correspondence after his trial, Sharpe displayed absolutely no remorse for killing Karen, still apparently blaming her for his predicament. Saying the divorce had driven him nuts, he attacked Karen for leaving him without any provocation. Sharpe blamed Karen and her lawyer Jacob Atwood for filing affidavits accusing him of everything from alcohol abuse to drug abuse, cross-dressing and physical abuse.

"All of this could have destroyed my medical career

and would have hurt my earning potential, but at the same time Atwood/Karen wanted me to support a 'Millionaire's' lifestyle for Karen," he said. "It made no sense. I was in a deep depression and could barely function, yet they kept pushing. Karen also made it very clear that she would also use all of this to take my kids away. Add eight medications, some alcohol and the ABANDONEMENT (sic) that I felt in the setting of severe depression and BPD (Borderline Personality Disorder) and the result I believe was a dissociative state or psychosis. Couple all this with literally stumbling across a gun and, well . . ."